Teenagers!

A
Bewildered
Parent's
Guide

Elizabeth Caldwell

Silvercat Publications
San Diego, California

Cover by Tyler Blik Design, San Diego, California.

10 9 8 7 6 5 4 3 2 1

Library of Congress Cataloging-in-Publication Data
Caldwell, Elizabeth, date
    Teenagers! : a bewildered parent's guide / Elizabeth Caldwell.
      p. cm.
    Includes index.
    ISBN 0-9624945-0-X (alk. paper)
    1. Parent and teenager—United States. 2. Teenagers—United
States. 3. Adolescent psychology—United States. I. Title.
HQ799.15.C35   1996   95-38761
305.23´5—dc20   CIP

Printed in the United States of America

Contents

1 Six Principles 5
Authority...6; Direction...7; Choice...8; Freedom...9;
Communication...10; Relationships...12; What's Next?...13

2 Authority 15
The Challenge Of Being Fair...16; Getting The Message
Across...17; Evolving Obedience...19; Ultimatums...21;
Coming to Terms with Authority...22

3 Direction 25
Role Models...26; Flexibility...28; Discipline...29;
Support...30; Self-Direction...31; Finding Common Ground...32

4 Choices 35
Choice: An Answerless Question...36; First Choices...36;
Clothing And Hair...37; *Friends*...39; *Food And Eating*...43;
Etiquette...45; *Homework*...47; Life, Liberty...And Choices...49

5 Freedom 51
The Call of the Wild...51; Freedom Is a Piece of Cake, Right?...53;
Preparing For Freedom...57; Freedom's Consequences...59;
Freedom And Responsibility...62

6 Communication 65
Don't Confuse Me with the Facts...66; Lipping Off...67;
Communicating With Teens...69; Teens Really Do Hear...71

7 Relationships 73
The Repeated Phrase Syndrome...74; Family Relationships...74;
Family Outings...76; Everyday Teen Friendships...80; The Opposite
Sex...83; Teachers And Teenagers...86; Just You And Me, Pal...87

8 Testing the Waters 89
What Testing Means...90; When, Where, And How...91; Rubber
And Concrete Steps...92; One-Liners...93; First Plunges...93;
Strategy...94; Points Of View...95; Warning Flags...96; Handling
Testing...96; *Testing And Rules: The Comic Book Convention*...97;
Testing And Failure: The Model United Nations...99; *Testing And
Responsibility: Phone Calls*...100; Let The Testing Begin!...101

9 Manipulation 103
Whittling Parents Down...104; The Passion Play...105; Playing On
Your Sympathy...106; The Fait Accompli...107; Divide And
Conquer...107; Relatives...109; Picking Fights...110;
Procrastination...110; Evasion...111; Dealing With Normal
Manipulation... 112; Conditioned Manipulation...115;
Unacceptable Manipulation...117

10 Privacy 119
The Room Syndrome...121; *Bathrooms*...121; *Bedrooms*...121;
Other Rooms...122; Privacy Outside...122; *Restaurants*...122;
Walks...123; Private Property...124; *Bookbags And School
Papers*...124; *Telephones*...125; *Mail*...126; Respecting
Privacy...127; Invading Privacy...129

11 The Teenage Playroom 135
The Teenager's Challenge...136; Adulthood Isn't Built in a
Day...139; Learning To Be Adults...140; Playrooms And
Relationships...143; Playrooms And Parents...145

12 Mistakes 149
Between Parent And Teen...149; Poor Judgment...150; Lack of
Knowledge...151; Inattention ...152; Mistake Quotas...153;
Other Mistakes...154; Compound Mistakes...155; Only Sweat
The Big Stuff...156

13 Good Teens, Bad Things 159
Drugs, Sex, Alcohol...160; Who or What Is in Control?...162;
Putting It In Perspective...164; Your Kid's On Drugs...166; Your
Responsibility...167

14 Some Parting Advice 169
Index 173

CHAPTER 1

Six Principles: An Overview

A teenager is a child who is turning into something resembling an adult. This is not an easy transition. For teenagers and parents alike, it is a difficult, challenging, and bewildering metamorphosis. The successful passage is usually an occasion for everyone involved to celebrate their liberation.

"What's going on?" your teenager wonders. "I'm big now. I've got an adult's body. I'm strong. I know everything I need to know to be a grown up. Nothing can go wrong. So why does everyone tell me I can't or shouldn't? I know more than they ever will!"

"What's going on?" parents mutter. "This kid thinks he knows everything at the age of someteen. ...She hasn't been around; she doesn't have the experience to know which end is up. She'll be lucky if she ever knows anything!...They think the world is some garden of Eden and that they are the center of the universe....He thinks he can march out and boss the world around just because he is beginning to feel his hormones."

"They just don't understand!" both cry out. With words like these they join the latest battle in the forever war between parents and teens. Each is the rain that falls on the other's picnic, the mole on the otherwise unblemished face of life.

It is not really that neither understands the other. In fact, each understands the other very well. The battles between teens and parents are fought on very well marked-out terrain. Kids and adults usually butt heads over those few basic principles that define what adult life is all about. Teens are learning these principles, though they often think they have already mastered them or that they don't need to. Parents are teaching these principles, though they may be teaching them in ways that no longer work. Both agree on the geography of the battle. Disagreements are more likely to occur over questions like where on the map the engagement is occurring or whether it is even necessary to be standing exactly there.

It is not unusual for parents and teens to fight the same battles, because most of the conflicts between parents and teens everywhere involve the same six principles: authority, direction, choice, freedom, communication, and relationships.

Authority

Teens need to learn about authority, about who is in charge. This is *not* to say that teens should be robots or zombies who slavishly obey the dictates of someone else. Teens must become independent and not stop thinking for themselves. But independence is not indulgence. Teens need to learn, as we all do, that there are times when they need to do what some appropriate other says to do.

Teens often have problems with issues of authority, because obeying someone else seems totally at odds with the autonomy that many feel is their birthright. They have spent most of their conscious lives doing what Mom and

Dad have told them to do. When they were five, it seemed perfectly natural. Now that they are someteen, it seems perfectly irritating. Teens often overreact, feeling that their years of abject subservience entitle them now to absolute liberty. They are adults, they believe, but they are still unfairly being treated like children. So, they want to break away from the control of their parents and to receive the respect and free-agency they feel suits their grown-up status. This is a proper goal. But before they can be autonomous, teens need to understand exactly how to balance the seeming conflicts between authority and autonomy.

These struggles often seem like tugs of war. The irresistible force meets the immovable object. Teen and parent hold their breaths, plant their feet, and glare across the chasm. Who is going to back down? Who is going to stand by their guns? Who is in charge? Both need to recognize that there are times to stand and there are times to back down. Teens need to learn that their parents are not simply trying to hold them back. Parents need to learn that teens are not going to do the goose-step simply because their parents demand it.

Direction

Who or what directs a teen's behavior? On the one hand, parents and others need to assert a certain amount of control. On the other hand, teens have to learn how to assume control of themselves. They need to accept direction from the outside in order to learn how to discipline themselves, while parents need to let go of the reins in order to discover that their kids don't need to be controlled.

Self-discipline is one of the qualities that measure how adult teenagers really are. The teenage transition takes children who may need to be prodded and turns them into adults who are able to govern themselves. As they learn self-discipline, teens can learn how to deny themselves, structure their behavior, say "no," or follow through. Unless teens learn how to discipline themselves, however, their lives are likely to be filled with frustrations, temper tantrums, resentments, demands for immediate gratification, and endless conflicts with parents.

Self-direction is one of the foundations of teenage self-esteem and one of the means by which teens learn to discipline, guide, and control themselves. For everyone, it is a milestone of liberation signaling that teens can be responsible for their own lives instead of being dependent on parents or others. The more teens can supply their own direction, the more parents and teens will benefit.

If only both parents and teens recognized this. In the tango that parents and teens dance, toes are often stepped on as both try to lead. Teens are like the blind men describing the elephant: they have no base of experience for knowing what self-discipline is. Parents can provide this direction if they can avoid becoming overbearing. They need to exhibit the very discipline they want their teen to master, backing off instead of overdisciplining for their own immediate gratification.

Choice

Teens also struggle to learn about choices and consequences. Most don't know how to make choices, because they have not yet had the life-experiences that enable adults to choose intelligently. Often, when they do make choices, they lack the sophistication to realize that choices are more than either/or decisions. By the time they are adults, most teens have learned that choices are made in a world of grays. Earlier in the teen years, most kids see only blacks and whites.

Teens need to be given every opportunity to make choices. They may not welcome the opportunity, especially when the alternatives are much more complicated than choosing between a hot dog and a hamburger. They need to learn that choosing is not easy, that choices have consequences, and that even bad choices do not mean the end of the world.

For their parts, parents should welcome the day when their teenagers can make intelligent choices, because that means parents no longer have to make as many decisions for their kids. Learning to choose, learning to make mistakes, and learning how to deal with the consequences—these are skills that help distinguish a kid from an adult. They are also qualities that free parents from the role of watchful guardian.

Freedom

Teens often look forward to the freedom that comes with growing up. Much less frequently do they recognize that freedom is inseparable from responsibility. Freedom seems like the credit card of life, the carte blanche to make whatever choices they want without having a parent or other adult looking over their shoulders or nagging in their ears. They may well forget that the credit-card statement comes every month and that freedom does not entitle them to ignore paying their bill.

Besides, it's a dangerous world out there. Most kids have grown up at least a little sheltered from the real world. As teenagers, they are only now developing the experiences and "street smarts" they need to exercise freedom intelligently. You probably do trust and respect your teen; so might the teachers, counselors, ministers, kids, and other adults that your teen has contact with. But most of this contact occurs with the understanding that you are there, standing behind your kid. Outside of this immediate circle, however, things are different. There are people out there who could and would eat your teen alive.

Teens don't always recognize this. As far as many are concerned, the world isn't like that, and even if it were, they are big enough or smart enough to keep the bad guys at bay. Parents know better, and teens need to learn better. The kinds of choices teens make tell their parents exactly how much freedom they are ready for. There is a big difference between choosing drugs, sex, gangs, or guns and choosing cars, sports, community service, or social relationships. The teen who chooses the latter can get into just as much trouble as the former, but the nature of the trouble is quite a bit different.

Teens are going to have their freedom, certainly at the age of majority if not earlier. How they exercise their freedom will depend, in part, on the lessons they learned during the years when their parents could make a differ-ence. Parents need to give their kids more rope as they show they are ready to have a larger radius of freedom. They may still abuse the liberty, but the teen years, under the watchful parent's umbrella, are the best time for kids to find out what the abuse of freedom can mean.

Communication

Communication is the skill that translates what goes on in the noggin into a form that others can understand. As teens mature, more goes on in their noggins. They have more to say, but they may not always feel like opening up. Parents may want to hear what their kids are saying, but they may not be willing to meet them where both can hear and understand.

Parents and teens have their own set of rules for communicating. These rules often seem different and contradictory. Parents often expect their kids to be a lot more logical and coherent than teens are ready, able, or willing to be. For their part, teens have their own language, one in which words, gestures, noises, clichés, and buzz-words all seem to be functionally equal. Parents need to recognize that a teenager's arsenal of communication includes such diverse things as finger-pointing, dramatic recreations, hyperbole, one-line quips, loud music, and bodily noises. Kids communicate this way in spite of their parents' objections, because they need to differentiate themselves from their elders, and something as fundamental as communication is a dramatic way of doing that.

Communication has a subsurface dimension as well. Frequently, it is not what you say but the way that you say it. Teens and parents alike expect that the other is going to shut up and listen when they are talking. There is an implied respect that both expect during times of communication. If one or the other even seems disrespectful, communication ceases and confusion, fear, or rejection take its place. "You're not listening to me!" is a symptom that communication really is breaking down.

Communication is never easy. But in the family as in life, it is essential that it be possible. Teens and parents may speak different languages at times, but that makes the need to learn a form of family Esperanto all the more important.

Unfortunately, it is parents who have to do most of the learning. Teens know how to speak parent-talk, because they have heard it ever since they were infants. On the other hand, teens cultivate their own lingo precisely because they want to have a language only they understand, one that most parents are not going to expend the time and effort to understand.

Relationships

Parents want to have good relationships with their teens. And teens want to have good relationships with their parents. Each may define a good relationship differently, but both are happier and more productive when they are parts of relationships in which they carry their own weights. As teens mature, they gain in weight, and their participation in the relationship needs to change accordingly.

A strong relationship is likely to cut across the other five principles. Authority and direction map out the realm of acceptable behavior. Choice and freedom allow for growth and evolution. Communication makes for two-way participation. Collectively, they form the common bonds that are implicit in the kind of family most parents want to have.

Relationships are never static. They expand and contract as parents and teens reach out and draw back. Parents will probably have many relationships with their teens. In part, this is because teenagers are evolving. One teen who has no problems with authority may not be ready for the freedom that his or her best friend enjoys. A year in the future, the same teen may have matured and left the friend far behind.

Teens, in turn, need to learn how to have relationships with others. This is not a skill that comes naturally. The transition from being the center of the universe to being one of many stars is not easy, but it is one every teenager needs to go through. Not that every one does. The world is full of former teenagers who have never lost the narcissism of their early childhood. But the more fully they master the principles behind relationships, the better able teens will be to form strong, healthy relationships of their own.

Your relationship with your teenager is a snap-shot of the condition of your parent-teen interactions. As your child matures, your relationship will be subjected to inevitable strains. While your teen wants more latitude and radical change, you may well seek to preserve your accustomed control and slow his or her progress. Whether the resulting friction causes irreparable damage or normal tension depends, in large measure, on how well all of you adjust to the changing nature of your relationship. This may be hard work, but it doesn't have to be the war that so many parents and teenagers turn it into.

What's Next?

What makes the teenage years seem so much like a struggle among titans is that the principles, while few in number, are crucial foundations of life. Teens must master these living skills if they ever expect to become responsible adults. Parents must help their kids learn the lessons if they are to carry out their responsibilities as parents.

The following chapters mark out some of the areas which are central to a teen's world. They are not intended to tell you how to raise your teen. Formulas and recipes for success in life exist by the zillions. There are any number of fine books you can read if you want to find out *what* to do.

This book is different. On the one hand, it is based on interviews with and first-hand observations of teenagers. Its stories and anecdotes really happened. Names, places, and some of the circumstances have been changed to protect the identities of the teens and their parents, and a few have been embellished a little to improve their telling, but the stories are all true. The few suggestions and recommendations in the book are included because they work, and they work because they balance the responsibilities of parents and the realities of teenagers. Finally, this book is "teen-tested." It has been read and evaluated by kids of all ages between nine and twenty-one. Their encouragement and feedback have contributed to this book far more fully than the experiences of a single parent possibly could.

Teenagers: A Bewildered Parent's Guide tells you what your teen is doing and why your teen is doing it. "Why does he do that?...What could she possibly be thinking?...How could they possibly imagine that it is all right?" Read on, and find out! When you are done, you will no longer be able to complain, "I'll never understand that kid of mine!" You may lose a favorite excuse, but you will also gain a much more realistic sense of the joys and challenges that you and your teenager have to look forward to.

CHAPTER 2

Authority

Fortunately for most parents, most kids learn something about authority long before they become teenagers. Up to adolescence (if not beyond), a child learns primarily by being given directions and shown examples by grown-ups and others. The child learns to accept that someone has authority and to respond appropriately when that authority is exercised. In these early years, this is Mommy and Daddy, the bosses of the world and the sources of all truth, justice, and power. The infant has to learn to obey when a parent says not to eat the discarded gum on the sidewalk or play with the lopping shears in the garage.

Ideally, a teenager has already learned to internalize obedience to appropriate authority. There is an intangible connection between parent and teen, one which helps delineate exactly where a teen's behavioral boundaries lie. The teen may fidget and squirm when faced with a need to comply, but the rules of the dialogue are already established. The teen has learned to trust the parent's judgment (at least in part), even when obeying the parent is uncomfortable or painful.

But that doesn't make dealing with authority any easier. Unfortunately, you, the parent, bear a disproportionate share of the burden. In order for your teen to trust your judgment or anyone else's, your demand for obedience must be reasonable and appropriate. Your teen doesn't have to understand your whys and wherefores (though you might prefer it), but your teen will recognize when you are arbitrary, inconsistent, or tyrannical. If you have to exercise authority, do it because what you want is good, not because what you want is what you want. Don't turn obedience into a dirty word.

The Challenge Of Being Fair

At times, you may need to be blunt. You may have to require unquestioned obedience. You may care if you seem despotic or tyrannical. *Do this!...Sit down!...Call me when you get there, or else!...Take the garbage out right now!...Listen to me!...You are grounded until your grades improve!...Stop hitting your sister this minute!*

Even at those times when you leave no room for compromise or negotiation, it is important that you have a good reason for what you tell your teen to do. Your teen may have difficulty hearing your demands—few teens like being told what to do by anyone, especially by a parent. Early in their teenage years, kids learn to equate obedience and subservience, and subservience of any sort is a no-no. Your ability to explain yourself might not make obeying any more palatable, but it will establish that you do have a reason. If that doesn't soothe your teen's sense of injustice, at least it will reassure both of you that you are not simply being contrary.

Teens do respond to fairness, though they may not be terribly happy about it. It was the day of the Senior Class picnic, and Janet had to let her sister Diane have the car. What a come-down! She had to get a ride with someone instead of driving up in her own wheels. Why did that little snit sister have to get the car? She was only going to drive to work, where the stupid car would sit parked all day.

"It's not fair!" Janet yelled. She threw the keys on the floor and stomped out of the kitchen. Her mother let Janet cool off a little, then sat down in the living room with her. "I am sorry you are so upset, but you need to understand a few things. First, it is not your car; we bought it for both of you. Second, a lot in life isn't fair, so get used to it. Third, I am not telling you to give Diane the car; I am asking you to because your sister needs to get to work. Finally, your friends aren't going to throw you to the wolves just because you have to get a ride from someone else. If they did, what kind of friends would they be? Look, we just can't afford cars for both of you."

Janet got the point. She was disappointed that she wouldn't be able to show off the car to her friends, but they knew about the car anyway. She was going to the picnic anyway. And, secretly, she was pleased that she wouldn't *have* to drive. "Okay," Janet said. "Diane gets the car for work. But it cuts both ways, right? Sometimes, I get the car."

"That's the whole idea," her mother agreed, quietly relieved that there would be no duel of honor the following sunrise.

Getting The Message Across

Paradoxically, admitting to your teen that you do not know everything can help to ease the agony of acquiescing to authority. You are human and you can make mistakes. But you have been around a little longer than your teen, so you do have some experience to draw on. Gently reminding your teen of this is one way of encouraging your teen to listen to what you are saying.

It still may not be easy to tell your seventeen- or eighteen-year-old teenager not to go out on a work-week night or to be back by eleven thirty so that Mom and Pop can turn the alarm on and go to bed. "Pick up your things!" and "Get out of bed right now!" are never easy to enforce.

You could use a gruff or commanding tone of voice to get your message across, but at what cost? Teens need to learn how to hear and respond to pleas for understanding and compassion. After all, it's not like you are telling them, as you did when they were young, to do something for reasons of health or safety. Most teens don't need to be told to look both ways before they cross the street or to wash their hands when they are done. By the time they are adolescents, kids more often need to be told about social skills. You are not trying to take their privileges away, but you are reminding them that they do not live on an island. It *should* make a difference that Mom or Dad needs to get up early the next morning to go to work or that Saturday is the only day they can sleep late.

Alan and his brother, Paul, were excited about the rifles they had received as birthday presents, especially when their father, Ralph, promised to take them hunting. On the morning of the big day, the three set out in the car, the brothers sharing visions of coming home with the entire deer population of the county on this, the day when they became real men.

The problem started when they got to the hunting stand. Alan thought that wearing the big, orange hunting vest was stupid. This was a hunting stand, he whined, not the open woods. Why should he have to put on the ugly, sissy vest? Ralph was equally adamant. Wear the vest...or else. He wasn't going to take the risk, because the conse- quences, as unlikely as they were, were too unthinkable. Paul was already wearing his. What was the problem?

For Alan, this was Bunker Hill and Gettysburg all rolled into one. He would not back down. Neither would Ralph. Wear the vest, or we go home. When Alan still balked, Ralph gathered up the rifles and vests, put them in the car, and told the kids to get in the car. Alan fumed, Paul sat in the back seat on the verge of tears, and Ralph muttered under his breath while he tried to soothe Paul's feelings.

Alan finally realized that he was ruining everyone's day, including his own. He didn't like backing down, but he recognized, if only for that moment, that he was not the only person in the world. "Okay, I'll wear your silly vest," he told Ralph. "Stop sniveling," he said to his brother. Alan began to learn the lesson of humility. There is no law, however, that says this lesson must be learned graciously.

Evolving Obedience

You may never need to say it in words, but always remember the essential fact: you are the parent. Most families have a pecking order, and the top perch usually belongs to the parents. (If your teen already occupies the cat-bird's seat, you may need more than this book can give you.) This arrangement keeps things working and allows you to carry out the responsibilities that go along with being a parent. Your teen needs to know where he or she fits in the hierarchy, to accept that place as much as possible, and to realize that this, too, shall pass as the teen becomes more mature. For the time being, though, it is as simple as this: it is your house and you make the ultimate decisions.

This doesn't make you the unquestioned lord of the manor. You can never be the all-powerful wizard, even though you may believe you deserve to be. Issues of authority are usually easier to resolve if you let your teen be part of the process. Sit down with your teen, talk over what you think needs to be said, and listen when he or she replies. Teens are not normally shy once they learn that it is okay to participate. They often want you to know up front exactly what they feel about the subject. They are apt to be especially animated if they feel you are compromising their freedom, rights, or turf.

Modern teens are going to speak their minds, whether you want to hear it or not. This is totally in keeping with what we have asked of our kids. "Learn how to be adults," we have told them. Part of being adults is being able to communicate.

Part of being adults is also being able to hear what your teen says. You may be shocked at what comes out of your teen's mouth, but the important point is that you are talking frankly, as equals. If your teen is able to trust that you are hearing with both ears, he or she is much more likely to accept the results by choice instead of necessity.

As your teen matures, all aspects of your relationship have to evolve. You need to be willing to change your expectations about things like obedience and conformity. Constructive conversations and your own attention to what is going on in your teen's life will tell you when it is time. Is it still reasonable to expect your child to follow the rules and regulations you laid down when your teen was little? Is he or she ready for more freedom and responsibility? What kinds of conflicts is your child facing to complicate the lines of authority? Is he or she mature enough to function without your being there all the time? What kind of peer pressure is your teen getting from friends and other teens? Your kid is growing older and more mature. All sorts of influences are pushing and pulling your teen in much more sophisticated directions. Your expectations about guidance and authority need to take these influences into consideration.

Ultimatums

A teen sometimes hears what a parent says as an ultimatum, even when it really *is* an ultimatum. An ultimatum is poison to healthy relations. After the words are said, the threat hangs in the air. It lurks behind events and conversations until the tension is resolved. An ultimatum reduces everything down to either-or, you-or-me, win-or-lose terms. You and your teen are backed into corners. You are forced to choose between two distasteful alternatives. If you enforce your ultimatum, you are a heavy. If you relent, you are a wimp. Your teen has to choose between defying you and risking your righteous anger or acquiescing and swallowing a big lump of pride.

No one likes an ultimatum. Neither parent nor teenager likes to have to choose between "my way" and "the highway." Between parents and children, the ultimatum rubs bare one of the constant sources of tension between generations: power. The parent doesn't ask, tell, or even command. The parent threatens physical, verbal, or psychological indignity. The teen, like the parent in the same position, wants only to respond with a simple "Drop dead!" and walk away. Sometimes the teen does, leaving the parents wondering what went wrong.

Ultimatums only work in simple, uncomplicated worlds where choices and alternatives are limited and predictable. The stakes are high, as Laurel and her parents found out. Laurel graduated from high school at the age of sixteen. She wanted to go to college, but she didn't feel ready for the emotional demands it would make. So, she decided to work for a while. She would start college when her friends graduated in a year or two. Her parents had a different idea. "Go to a community college first, then you can transfer when your friends graduate," they said. "We'll buy you a car, new clothes, pay your tuition, anything you want." Still, Laurel said "No."

Laurel got a job in retail sales and moved into her own apartment. She liked the work and did well enough that her manager offered her a place in the company's two-year management training program. Laurel was ecstatic. "Yes," she replied. "No," her parents insisted. "That is like throwing your life away on a job that anyone can do. If you take that training program, don't come back home, and don't ask us for help, either." She took the job, in part because of her parents' ultimatum, and had to find out how to live in the adult world without help at the age of sixteen. Laurel and her parents learned what can happen when an ultimatum is issued.

Coming to Terms with Authority

As they get older, teens ask more and more for respect. They increasingly believe that they deserve to be treated as autonomous individuals, and they expect their parents to acknowledge that they are proficient, knowledgeable, and capable. A lot of parents would be surprised to learn that their teens are right.

For example, one day I awoke with intense stomach pain, and my doctor told me to meet him at the hospital. My son helped me into the passenger's seat and took his place behind the wheel. "You've got to trust me," my teen said as we pulled into the street. "I know you don't believe me, but I really don't need you to give me directions. I know what to do, so just let me do it." He was right, and I didn't feel much like nagging. We got there in plenty of time after making only a few wrong turns.

You can still ask your teen to do something, and the chances are good that it will get done. But you can't simply demand compliance. At some point, most teens learn to take direction because they choose to, not because they have to. You need to let the shift take place and get ready for the day when "just because I said so" is no longer a sufficient reason. In fact, that day may already be here.

You have to trust that your teen will learn how to deal with authority. You have raised your child from diaper days in the best way you could. Perhaps you made some mistakes—who hasn't?—but you provided your teen with a basis for responding to the world. Even though your teen is no longer a small child, that base of behavior is still there. Everything you have done is not about to evaporate. Encourage your child to build on that foundation, not tear it down.

CHAPTER 3

Direction

It is not always easy for them, but teens have to learn how to take control of their own lives, to develop a structure of self-discipline that they can use for the rest of their lives. When they are small, their direction usually comes from the outside. Parents impose discipline on younger children to make sure they follow certain rules or behave in a certain way. This external discipline works best when kids are younger, more pliable, and less assertive.

Eventually, kids learn to replace the external direction of their parents with their own internal discipline. Parents spend less time imposing order as teens learn how to regulate and control their own lives. This internal direction guides just as effectively as external direction, but it is the teenager, not the parent, who decides which path to follow. Teens learn the paradox that self-discipline creates freedom, independence, and autonomy, precisely because it confines behavior within "acceptable" boundaries where so much more is possible.

Teens typically want the freedom to discipline themselves. They fluctuate in their abilities to impose self-discipline, however, so parents have to be ready to reassert their guidance. As teens develop their ability to control themselves, parents have less need to be intimately involved, even when they don't necessarily approve of the paths their teens have chosen to follow. Parents, for their part, need to recognize when their teens become able to exercise internal discipline and to modify their external discipline accordingly. By overcontrolling, parents can actually slow their teens' progress toward adulthood.

Role Models

Direction can be as simple as inspiration. As one teen told me, "I've always looked up to my mother. If I can only be just like her! She achieved her goals by working hard and ignoring all the people who told her that women couldn't become chemists. It just wasn't done. Well, she proved them wrong, didn't she?"

Parents can do a lot of inspiring simply by being good role models. A positive example offers something to work toward and a diagram for getting there. Of course, "there" has to be someplace the teen wants to get, and the teen has to make that decision. You can't just tell your kid to be like you and expect that stars will fill his or her eyes. But you don't need to expect that your teen will follow your path toward fame and fortune. Even such simple courtesies as generosity, understanding, politeness, and consideration can be taught by example.

Unfortunately, parents can also be negative role models. Insensitivity, disrespect, abuse, and violence can leave teens feeling angry, frustrated, and resentful and legitimize a style of behavior that repeats itself later when they become parents themselves. This is what happened to Jerry, an otherwise respected businessman who overdisciplined his two teens, Nicky and Kevin, with physical punishment. He slapped and pinched Nicky and took the belt to Kevin. Why? Because his parents had done the same to him, and he simply treated his kids the way he was treated by his parents. He used corporal punishment to command their attention, to control them, to keep them from getting away with something, and to let them know he meant business.

Unfortunately, what Nicky and Kevin learned was that they were powerless to stop what they knew was abusive behavior. Throughout their teen years, they felt incapable of standing up for themselves. Their only recourse, they learned, was to do things behind authority's back and spend lots of creative energy finding ways to avoid getting caught.

Jerry's attempts to impose direction were excessive. Brute force is seldom an acceptable solution to simply personal problems. Jerry extracted obedience (if you could call it that) at the expense of Nicky's and Kevin's self-esteem. He substituted pain and hurt for guidance and leadership. And he left the teens with a sense of inadequacy and a dubious but indelible formula for disciplining others.

Jerry never questioned the message he was sending. In fact, he defended it. He wore the scars on his own arms and legs proudly—they "proved" he was a man. He was a responsible citizen only because his parents made sure he got what he deserved. If it was good enough for him, he said, it was good enough for Kevin and Nicky. It was the only way to control their wild and outlandish behavior. They'd thank him one of these days.

Maybe so and maybe not, but Jerry would have been well-advised to question just what kind of role he was modeling. It is important that parents, as role models, help guide their teens through the teen years. These are difficult enough years without excursions down paths that lead nowhere.

Flexibility

A teen's developing sense of direction provides a framework for discovering strengths and weaknesses, experimenting with choices, and learning from mistakes. Teens continue to grow if their parents are perceptive enough to allow them to grow toward directing their own lives. Flexible parents can share the burden with their teens, stepping in when the situation requires it and stepping back at other times. Flexible guidance is cooperative guidance, because it encourages parents and teens to work together.

Rosie felt that her parents didn't trust her. "They said they only wanted the best for me, but then they always turned around and said, 'No, you're too young.'" She seethed at the curfew, at the leashes on her social activities, at the restrictions on her dating. Even getting a job at a local mall didn't seem to help; her mother insisted on chaperoning her to and from work.

Rosie was not willing to recognize the only thing her parents could see. She *was* young. She *was* inexperienced. She didn't have the street smarts to be free of the leash. Her parents were concerned that she would get in over her head if they did not exercise some kind of supervision. Perhaps they were a little too watchful, but they made it clear to Rosie that any errors they made would be on the side of caution.

Fortunately, they were willing to meet each other half-way. Rosie proposed a compromise: if she found a job closer to home and a ride to work with a fellow employee, could she go to work unchaperoned? Her parents agreed. Rosie found the job, got the ride, gave her parents a copy of her schedule, and reassured them that they could call her at work. When the new arrangement proved successful, Rosie and her folks renegotiated their deal. Rosie got a second-hand car. Her mother stopped calling her at work. As she proved herself capable of handling her job, her parents relented in other areas as well. Within a few months, Rosie was handling her social life and staying out late enough to enjoy both dinner *and* a movie.

Rosie and her folks worked out a way to balance the needs of both. Rosie was allowed to grow according to her own direction, and her parents were allowed to relax their vigilance. She learned the skills to pursue her own goals and the rewards that come from initiative. They learned that they really didn't have to control their child forever. Everyone gained from being flexible.

Discipline

Discipline is part of a parent's attempt to provide guidance. To be effective, it has to address what is going on right now. For the parent, discipline that is not driven by a connection to actual circumstances is discipline for its own sake. If teens are to learn self-discipline, they have to discover the virtues of responding to the world as it is, not as their parents might want it to be.

When parents do act, they need to take actions that teens will take seriously. Steps like grounding them for life, taking away their car keys for six months, or denying them phone privileges for years make little impression. Most teens consider these just parts of the game, disruptions that will blow over in a while even if they can't get around them right now. These are not meaningful acts, because they are not real. These are the acts of parents who are desperate to get back at their teens for something and symptoms of a relationship in which timely and relevant interactions have been replaced by something else.

Parents can intervene much more effectively when what they do is related to the behavior that makes it necessary. Appropriate discipline should fit the crime and come as a natural consequence of a teen's actions. Grounding Sarah "for life" simply because she stayed out after curfew one time might be excessive and unenforceable, but grounding her for a specific length of time because she had taken too many liberties with her freedom might be appropriate. Locking up Roger's car keys because he forgot to turn in his homework might be extreme, but it might be totally proper if Roger had neglected his homework because he spent too much time cruising the front and back roads of the neighborhood.

Discipline works when it calls attention to the problem and its consequences. If it gets to the point where your teen turns it into a game of getting away with something, you have already lost the battle. If your teen can get away with it when the discipline comes from you, what is going to happen when your teen needs to discipline himself or herself? The best alternative is action that teens understand and respond to. This teaches even when it punishes.

Support

Parents often look at their teens in us-versus-them terms and view discipline as something done *to* someone. In reality, guidance is much more a give-and-take. Kids are always going to do things that call for discipline. They make mistakes and misjudgments and sometimes leave their brains on top of the dresser when they set out to do something. Many parents simply judge and punish when their kids goof. Often, however, kids need the understanding and support that demonstrate what parents can never compel.

Sometimes, the best thing to do is nothing at all. When Jack woke up in the hospital, he knew the accident had been his fault. He waited for his parents' ax to come down on his neck. But all they did was tell him that the car didn't matter as long as he was okay. Jack didn't need their help to think about the accident or the car he totaled. Perhaps if his folks had nagged, he would have tuned them out and lived to crash the car again. Instead, he punished himself and learned a valuable lesson.

Most teens are like Jack. They know when they mess up, and they often start punishing themselves in their own ways long before Mom and Dad get around to it. Teens don't need you to tell them they have done something wrong.

Discipline needs to be built on a foundation of respect and support. There is at least as much to be said—and probably a lot more—for positive reinforcement. Teens need to be told when they have done something well. And they need to know that you are there for them even when they do something badly. Screwing up by accident and screwing up on purpose are different things. Your discipline needs to recognize this difference.

Self-Direction

What teens frequently need from you is the space to take care of their problems themselves. Most teens realize that they will remain shackled to you as long as you are in charge. They will always want to be free of your control, but at some point they become willing to take on the responsibility of directing themselves.

Teens reach this point when they realize that they *can* discipline themselves. Not all teens achieve this enlightenment at the same age, and most teens are inconsistent in their ability to regulate themselves. But almost all teens wake up one morning and realize that they are not passive agents in the world. Once they recognize this, their lives are never the same again.

It helps if teens have goals to stimulate their self-discipline. When my son had a goal, he turned from being a catch-as-catch-can, typically lazy teenager into a focused crusader. He knew what he wanted and set his sights accordingly.

"Hey, Mom," my teen announced one day. "I have a chance to be an exchange student in Thailand next summer. Can I go?"

"That's wonderful, Hon," I replied, "but I can't afford to send you. I feel terrible."

"Mom, I know we don't have the money. But listen to this: there's a scholarship I can get—I went to the library and found out all about it. If you say it's okay, I can get a job to cover the rest of the costs. Mr. Hayes down at the Food Lot already said he'd let me bag groceries. Please say it's okay."

I gave my approval. "Thanks, Mom! By the way, I started work yesterday."

Finding Common Ground

Teens may never enjoy being disciplined by others, and parents (despite what some teens may believe) will never relish cracking the whip. But the issue of who is in control doesn't have to cause problems between parents and teenagers.

Always encourage a dialogue with your teen. You are the parent, but that doesn't necessarily make you right about everything. You are there as a guide to help, not as a czar to dominate or control. Your teen is a unique individual, a person who has something to say and something to offer. Recognize that you may not be able to be objective about what your teen is saying or doing. Be humble.

Give your teen a chance to exercise self-direction. Your teen will tell you, perhaps even before you are aware of it, that if you keep on doing all the doing, your child will never learn how to do for himself or herself. If you try to provide all the direction, you will spoil your teen and discourage your child from learning how to do it without help. When your teen eventually needs to exercise self-discipline, he or she may not know how and just blame the world for his or her own failings. You can only be constructive if you offer something your teen can reuse.

Turn your discipline into a form of feedback that enhances self-esteem. You are in charge, but let your teens have a say in what your discipline should be. Help him or her grow from the experience by making sure your teen understands what he or she did and why you have to get involved. Help your teen learn from mistakes.

Don't react every time something goes wrong. Most of the time, your teen will know it before you do. Save it for the times that really need your attention, and make whatever you do proportional to the problem needing correction. Your intervention has to serve a purpose. If it is just a "filler," it will do little beyond wasting time.

You and your teen share a two-way street. Parental involvement is not a weapon against recalcitrant offspring. Nor is it an obstacle in a teenager's game of keep-away. Rather, discipline, direction, and guidance form a bridge connecting you with your teen. Parents can influence and encourage their child's passage to independence and adulthood, while kids can learn about life from their parents' words and deeds. Balancing the needs and responsibilities of both parents and teens makes the world a better place for everyone.

CHAPTER 4

Choices

Choices. Teens make a lot of them, good ones and bad ones. Sometimes, we wish that our teens would never make any choices. At other times, we encourage them to make as many choices as possible.

Parents make a lot of choices too, but parental choices are different. Most parents take care to base their choices on judgment, skill, and discrimination. Parents' choices usually include paying attention and taking care, whereas teenagers often seem to give as much attention to making choices as they'd give to choosing between vanilla and strawberry. They don't always exercise much thought or introspection. Teens just choose randomly and impulsively.

Before the end of their teenage years, most kids learn how to choose intelligently. Fortunately, the choices teenagers make are not always catastrophic or life threatening (though they can be), but the results are not always what they hope for. Kids can learn from their successes and failures and from the results when they make their choices. They can learn on the job, so to speak. There are times when they can even exercise the option of not choosing. This is a luxury. By the time they are adults, it is no longer an option.

As parents, one of our primary tasks is to make sure that our kids know how to make intelligent choices. Why? The simple fact is that teens who make choices become more mature, independent, and adept in handling their own affairs than teens who never take on the challenge.

Choice: An Answerless Question

For the typical teenager, choices are confusing. When asked or told to choose, many teens don't know what to say. Their vague responses to our questions— *yes...no...maybe...perhaps...uh*—become screens to mask their confusion. They may become cryptic and argumentative—*Whose life is it?...What do you want from me?...Whom do you think you are making choices for?*

Parents who are unable to fathom their teen's confusion or the choices their kids make often demand still more choices. *Where are you going?...What time are you coming home?...You're going out looking like that?...Do we get to meet the parents?*

Baffled, both teens and parents face off, waiting for someone else to answer the questions, make the decisions, and move on to the next parental-teen crisis. *I can't decide. Should I wear this pair of shoes or should I color my hair green? What do you think?*

Irritation, indecision, bragging, triumph—whatever is required of the teen at that exact moment. Just don't ask the impossible. Making choices is...like...huh... well...you know...difficult...know what I mean?

First Choices

Initiating teens into the mysteries of choice-making is troublesome for many parents. I started my teen when he was four. He wanted a stuffed animal and a candy bar. I had money only for one of them. He had to choose. The

man standing in line behind us was shocked. How could
I be such a mean mother? Imagine! Forcing this young and
tender child to make such a choice! My son chose the
candy bar. Oh well.

At nineteen things hadn't changed much for my teen.
Making choices was still an agonizing chore. (I don't exactly leap at every opportunity to choose, either.) But at
least he had his teenage years to draw on for experience.

Some of the typical areas where teenagers begin to
make choices are discussed below.

Clothing And Hair Don't expect your teen's choices
about clothes and hair to be like yours. One day, your teen
is going to make a fashion statement. Watch out! I can still
hear that salesperson's voice ringing in my ears.

"You're going to let him buy this?" He flashed a gaudy
shirt in front of my eyes.

To the salesperson, my son had obviously made the
wrong choice. I didn't see it the same way. I was not the
one who was going to wear the gaudy shirt (maybe my teen
was going to tone it down with black or beige pants). I
thought it was important for my teen to be allowed to
select his own clothes without parental interference.

Clothing is one of the teen's first statements about
himself or herself. It is important to let our kids express
themselves. Clothes express teens' understandings of
who they are and the importance they give to their sense
of themselves. We should be very careful about confronting our teens over their clothing.

(This is true only up to a point. Many types of teens'
clothes now make social statements which help teens
project their emotions to the rest of the world. Anti-war,
political, or religious messages may seem responsible applications of the freedom of expressions; messages extol-
ling drugs or gang identities may not. Discuss with your

teen what his or her particular clothes are saying to the world-at-large. Your teens might not be ready to confront the realities of such a decision. Not all teens are trying to engineer political rebellion or social justice. Some teens just like to dress differently. It sets them apart from the herd. Still, wearing bell bottom pants with a gaudy shirt and beads conveys hippie and druggie culture whether or not your teen is on drugs or flower power.)

By their own choices, my teen's friends wore clothes which ranged from the strange and weird to the conservative and conformist. A lot depended on the fashion and personality statements they were making at that particular moment of that particular year.

One friend wore "straight" clothing. He was very conservative: marine haircut, buttoned cotton shirts, muted pants, and black penny loafers. He also wore T-shirts with images of heavy metal rock groups.

Another wore painted jeans and ecology T-shirts and pinned Swiss chard in his hair. On occasion, he wore a black hooded robe with unlaced black combat boots.

Other teens seem determined to make their statements by avoiding making choices. I knew some teenagers who always wore the same pair of pants with the same shirt or the same kind of skirt with the same blouse. They resisted wearing anything else, and, by virtue of their choices, spent a great deal of time washing their clothing.

My teen wandered from the conservative to the grotesque, depending on his mood and how much he wanted to shock me. (That is part of the equation, too. Teens instinctively know what will annoy, anger, or frustrate their parents when it comes to clothing.)

He went through several stages. It started with the black stage. He had to wear everything black—black shirts, black sweaters, black pants, and black socks.

From the black stage, he progressed to the white stage. Everything he wore was white.

The next stage was multi-color: black, white, and purple!

None of this really bothered me. It wasn't any of my business. He, not I, wore the clothing. I had to respect and trust his judgment. If he liked what he wore, who was I to get in his way? I imposed only minimal limits. He could wear whatever he wanted, provided that he stayed out of trouble, came home with good grades, created his own fashions and not someone else's, and did his own white laundry.

I listened to what my teen was telling me. He wanted to create his own sartorial identity. It would have been easy to get caught up choosing clothing for him or picking up something handsome or macho for him at the mall. Many teens won't accept that anymore (if they ever did). They want to be asked or consulted first. They may want to wear exact replicas of what their friends wear or whatever is advertised as the thing to wear that season. Otherwise, they wouldn't be caught dead in it.

The same can be said about hair styles. When teens choose to cut, dye, or shear their hair in an unconventional manner, society may equate that hair style with a political or social movement. Make sure your teen understands the consequences of these choices, too. Then let your teen concentrate on being himself or herself.

Friends They come with the neighborhood, school, activity, or church. They're whomever your teen chooses for pals, life-long buddies, back-up support systems, emotional screams, and talk-a-thons. They may not fit your expectations about your kid's friends. But unless you feel *strongly* that a particular friend means potential trouble down the line, allow your teen the opportunity to choose his or her own friends. Whomever your teen selects, it's not your call, whether or not you approve.

Among teens, friendships begin as eternal bonds. Their friends are extremely important to them-whether these friends stay within expected behavioral bounds or not. Allow your teen the sadness of learning how short eternity is and the pleasure of discovering who is there at the end. It's not up to parents to decide. It's up to your teen. Friends who once were tight may drift off suddenly, and merely okay friends may wind up as firm and fast buddies throughout the teenage years.

When my teen passed from junior high to high school, many of his old friends didn't make the transition quite as smoothly as my teen did. He matured over the summer and began taking responsibility for his actions. I wasn't pleased that many of his friends didn't. His friends couldn't fit in new situations (junior or senior high) or couldn't adjust to what was happening around them (older sibling moving out, parents divorcing, grandparents moving in, deaths in the family). In response to these changes they reacted unpredictably. Still, my teenager chose to remain faithful to his friends. He made sure his friends understood that he would not abandon them just because they did not meet his mother's expectations.

One of these friends was Jonas. All his life Jonas's parents had worked. He had an older sister who took care of and looked out for him. It was an arrangement that suited everyone. Someone forgot that one day big sister would leave for college. When she left, change came abruptly.

My son came home from school one day and announced; "Guess what Jonas is up to?"

"What?" I asked.

"He cut his hair," my teen announced solemnly.

"Well, that's not so bad. All teens cut their hair," I said.

"It's not what you think. It's a lot more than that. Jonas shaved off all his hair on the right side, and on the left side, he clipped the hair halfway up his head."

"Okay, he's extreme," I replied.

"No! You still don't understand," my teen paused. "Jonas wears a double set of bike chains around his neck. He wears car chains around his body."

"Must be heavy to carry around," I choked out.

"He's also dressing in leather. And, he took a blow-torch and graffitied the school walls with obscenities."

I didn't say anything. My teen and Jonas still hung out together. Friends do that. They don't desert one another when times get tough...unless one or both of them decide to. Eventually my teen decided he just couldn't handle Jonas's antics by himself. One day Jonas came home with my teen. The next week Jonas was banished. My teen left Jonas behind in junior-high-school time and went on with his own life. (Yes, I was pleased).

My teen didn't expect me to understand his choice to stand by Jonas or his later choice to cut him loose. He did expect me to go along with his decisions and not interfere. My teen chose to go ahead without Jonas. I assume this was fine with Jonas, too. I never saw him again, nor did my son ever mention Jonas's name, even when other friends did.

Peter was another friend. He and my teen went back to second grade. They were terrific pals and inseparable. One day my son came home and told me that Peter had chosen to "dead-out" at fourteen. He wasn't doing well in school, had fights with his father, and thought life was a bummer. He found some new friends who handled life by standing around the mall drinking. For Peter, it was easier to settle into obscurity than to move on.

My teen tried to stand by his old friend. The choice was difficult because my son didn't drink or like to bum around malls. It was Peter who finally chose to break up the friendship and pushed my teen away. I couldn't make that choice for my son, even though I wanted to. My teen had to learn how to deal with these things by himself, on his own terms and at his own pace.

Pushed away by Peter and stunned by Jonas's life changes, my son had to make other choices about his best friend, Michael. Michael had been a good kid who always stood by my teen. They played electronic games together and often engaged in deep philosophical discussions. They also shared the burden of being intellectuals in a sports-minded school and neighborhood.

My teen didn't care. Michael did. He deliberately flunked seventh grade, then he flunked summer school. He achieved his wish. Michael was placed in mainstream classes with "normal" friends.

Again, my teen was placed in a quandary. Should he remain friends with Michael or was it time for him to move on? The decision was made for him. Michael didn't want any smart friends around. My teen would have remained friends. He didn't care about a person's smarts, abilities, or gifts. He wanted the friendship for its own sake. But he wasn't about to flunk all his classes just to remain friends with Michael or to fit in socially with other kids his age. My teen made the decision to remain on his own road and not to allow outside influences or peer pressure to influence his choices.

Friendship choices are some of the most significant early choices your teen will have to make. Many teens don't feel comfortable making them. Parents don't help if they send double messages. *It's okay. I like this one. It's not okay. They're going to be trouble makers.* Teenagers are no longer making little-kid choices. Smaller children may have to consider nothing more serious than *Do they like me?...Will they play ball or house with me?...Will I be invited to their party?* Teens find themselves preparing for more nearly adult kinds of choices. *Should I go along with the gang even though I don't want to?...I don't want to study all weekend, but I will fail if I don't....Should I go out Friday night or stay home with sibling Jane or Joe?*

Teenage friendship is a serious matter, one that shouldn't be taken lightly by any parent. Tread carefully where friends are concerned. Before you jump in, put things in perspective. Try to remember your own teenage years. How did you feel when your parents tried to call the shots? How did you react to your parents decisions? How did you handle ultimatums? Did you defy them? Did your parents allow any exceptions? Did you go behind their backs to meet your friend anyway? Did your own parents' judgments affect your relationship with your friends?

Do you really expect your teen to act any differently? How would you handle the situation today if you were a teenager? If you acted like your parents did, would things be any different, and if so, what would the difference be? Does your explanation sound right to you and your teen (be honest)?

Teens will make and nurture friendships with or without your approval. Perhaps your teenager will ask your opinion. If so, be there. Discuss with your teen what you feel is right or wrong about this friend and why. Communicate your feelings, but don't try to dictate. Trust that your teen's choices will work out for the best about as often as parent's choices do. Which is most of the time.

Food And Eating Most parents have introduced their teens to the four basic food groups. But teenagers develop their own standards of good nutrition. Somewhere during their teenage years, kids learn that they can make choices about what they eat, when they eat, and how they eat. Unfortunately, only a few teenagers make broccoli or spinach their first choices.

Sometimes their choices border on the absurd. I know of one home in which the mother prepares two and a half separate meals for her family. One teen eats vegetables and drinks juices. The other teen eats meat, potatoes, and drinks cola. The parents eat what's left over from their teens' plates. The parents have given their teens excessive power of choice at meal time. No one sits down and eats at the same time. Meals are hectic.

This may be an extreme example, but few families are immune. I realized I was in trouble one day when my teen announced he had no time to sit at the table and eat. I was not too pleased with this particular choice and asked him to explain. The logic behind his choice was air-tight: four out of five teens don't sit down and eat supper with their family. It's just not done that way. "You should be honored that I sit down and eat dinner with you at all."

The reasons behind his other food choices were equally indisputable:

"I don't like salad. But I'll eat some carrots, lettuce, and sunflower seeds, if you insist."

"I'll only eat: pizza; fried chicken; corn bread; French fries; milk shakes; egg rolls; sushi and sashimi; Chinese food; peanut butter and jelly sandwiches; anything you bake, Mom; steak; hamburgers; milk; orange juice; and pistachio or any other kind of nut. And 'eating- out' food."

"You can't make me. There's no law that says I must eat this. So there."

You can't force teens to regard eating as a family activity or to change their minds once they've made them up. Nevertheless, you can still encourage your kids to think about what they are eating and to continue regarding themselves as part of the family. For example:

☞ Don't simply issue orders. Find out what your teen's schedule is for the evening, week, and month, and take it into consideration. Inform your teen of what your plans are. Let your teen see that you are trying to coordinate the two schedules.

☞ If your teen is involved in sports or other events, schedule meals around these occasions. Stress that this is an important meal for everyone.

☞ Emphasize that you are still a family and that dinner is the one meal at which everyone should sit down to together.

☞ Have your teen choose two nights out of the week and plan to be present at dinner at least on those two nights.

☞ No distractions during dinner! No running off to watch television or splitting from the house until everyone is done eating. No phone calls before, during, or right after dinner. If the phone rings, don't answer it, or let the answering machine do the work. If the doorbell rings, you answer it.

☞ Set an example. You follow these rules, too. Your teens will follow your actions even if they're unwilling at first.

Etiquette Some teens have it. Others don't. Still others have it and choose not to use it. My teen turned his on and off according to how he felt that day. It all depends...like most things with teens.

My teen came home from school one day with a note. It seems that he had been too polite. He'd been opening the school doors for girls, older people, and handicapped persons. He was pulling out seats, taking coats and hanging them up, and answering respectfully in class.

This was too much for one substitute teacher who thought my teen was sucking up to her. She kicked him out of the class and told him to sit in the hallway and reflect on his evil ways.

One of the hall monitors, Mr. Finn, came over and asked what the problem was. My teen explained it to him. Soon he and my teen were talking in loud voices with fists pounding on the school walls to emphasize what acceptable behavior was.

The substitute came out to investigate. My teen got up from his chair, apologized, and suggested that he be sent to the principal. The substitute turned bright pink. Mr. Finn coughed and left. My teen was indeed sent to the principal, who ordered him to write one hundred times for homework that he would not be so polite in the future.

No wonder teenagers find manners confusing.

For many adults, etiquette hasn't been practiced since Fred Astaire stopped making movies. Many of us don't exercise it as often as we should, either. When a teenager chooses to use good manners, suspicious adults often look to find hidden motives. Still, we continue to hope that one day our teens will learn that practicing good manners is a good thing.

It is not that difficult to instill an appreciation of etiquette. Try some of the following:

☞ Teach your teenager the basics of etiquette—pull out a chair, help someone with a coat or jacket, offer to carry a package.

☞ Remind your teenager to keep his or her mouth shut while someone else is speaking. If your bluntness doesn't work, try this. When your teen starts telling about an event, project, or other thing of importance, start a loud conversation of your own with your spouse or a friend. See how your kid likes competing with you. Experience is a

good teacher. Your teen should learn the lesson quickly and remember to keep silent while others are speaking.
☞ Encourage your teenager to practice good manners. Give as many gentle reminders as you need to. Remind them that "what goes around, comes around" and that "one of these days it will happen to you." If you stress it often enough, your teen will tune in and hear what you're saying.
☞ Practice good manners yourself. *You* chew with your mouth closed and *you* use language correctly. Demonstrate the respect for and consideration of others that you want your teen to show. Your example will be remembered, even if reluctantly.

Homework Choices about doing homework? In some schools, homework seems to have joined the inkwell in the what-did-they-ever-use-this-for? archives. Yet, many teens insist that homework still exists. They swear they have no choice.

Teens don't have to tell us that doing homework is a drag. It wasn't that long ago when we had homework, too. Most teens have their horror stories. One teen told me about her choice to do homework with her friend and how it backfired.

"I had a test the next day and received permission from my parents to go study with a friend. When I got there we started studying, but we were hungry. We decided to go out and get something to eat.

"The next thing I know, I'm in big trouble. My parents decided to check up and they called my friend's house to make sure that I was studying. When they heard that my friend and I had left to eat, my Father got into his car and searched for me. He spotted my car, and left. When I got home, he accused me of lying...as if I hadn't planned on studying at all.

"The results were disastrous. My parents said they could no longer trust me. They made me feel as if I didn't exist. It's been like that for three weeks. We're almost talking again."

This happens occasionally. A choice your teen has made somehow goes awry. Parent and teen will always miscommunicate, and not only about homework. This simply reinforces the importance of good communication between you and your teenager.

Before you lose control over your teenager's style of studying, take some of the following steps:

- Have your teen explain homework and studying plans explicitly, even when they include trips to the Burger Barn, radio or television breaks, or taking a hike.
- Understand that most teens become easily distracted. It's part of their genetic make-up. No amount of yelling or screaming will bring them back. Expect it and don't become rattled. The homework gets done—eventually—at the teenager's own pace.
- Be tolerant of peculiar study styles. Many teens require radios, television, tape recorders, CD players, and other noise sources while they study (or at least they think they do.) Teens study in a variety of positions: lying down, reclining, slouching, propped up on elbows. Desks may not even be considered appropriate.
- Understand that long phone conversations may actually stimulate an information exchange.
- Recognize that attention spans vary. Many teens do homework in increments of seconds rather than minutes or hours. Most teens do intend to complete their homework, but you need to recognize that procrastination is a given.
- Not all homework is done at home under your watchful eyes. Many if not most teens do homework during homeroom period, right before classes, during free periods, and

on the bus. (Some do none at all, but this is a completely different problem.)

Teens may not like to take responsibility for their actions, including doing or not doing their homework. It's a lot easier for teens to say "No, I'll do it later" than to make the choice to hit the books right away. Unless they think it is to their advantage, teens will often take the easy way out.

Yet responsibility cannot be shirked. What differentiates choices about homework from other types of teenage choices is the immediacy of the consequences. The instant feedback supplied by a conscientious teacher whose homework assignment was ignored should offer your teen a valuable lesson: choice and responsibility cannot be separated.

Life, Liberty...And Choices

Teenagers are going to make choices, whether we approve or not. They consider the right to choose one of the inalienable rights which they will defend, in their own romantic fashion, unto death (theirs or ours).

We cannot expect every choice our teens make to be a good one. Learning to choose intelligently is as much a trial-and-error process as learning algebra or driving. Some of their choices will be terribly misinformed. Others will be grossly selfish. A few will be simply bad. It is the only way to master a new skill.

As parents, we can help our teenagers through this learning process by encouraging them to make choices and experience the consequences. Focus on the act of choosing, not on the outcome. Stand behind them as they choose, even when we wish with all our passion that they would choose differently. If we see our kids making dangerous or harmful choices, we certainly should intervene.

Otherwise, back off and let them experience the lesson that choices cannot be made without repercussions.

Encourage your teens to choose with an eye toward the consequences of their choices. Being responsible for one's actions is one of the things that differentiates most grown-ups from their children. Learning to accept responsibility is not easy, but it is an essential step in the successful progression from teenager to adult. Once learned, responsibility is a lesson that they will keep for the rest of their lives.

When your teen is ready to begin making choices, stand by him or her and encourage your child to choose, even when it is difficult. The best you can do for your teenagers is to teach them to make sound judgments, and then learn to trust those judgments. They will learn from the frustration and pain how to choose wisely.

CHAPTER 5

Freedom

When they are young, children mill around you, dogging your legs, slapping your hands, and otherwise letting you know that their existence depends on continual physical contact. Those days come to an immediate end as soon as your child becomes a teenager. Dependence is replaced, not by what we might call independence, but by what a teenager calls freedom.

The Call of the Wild

The quest for freedom usually begins when a teenager embraces personal mystery. Teenagers learn quickly that keeping their parents guessing is a good thing. Freedom becomes confused with inscrutability. No decent teenagers would think of allowing their parents the security of a stable or staid routine.

Most teenagers keep their parents in the dark in one of two ways. Some make their lives appear as a patchwork quilt. The pieces are all there, but the assembly seems haphazard. Everyone in the family tries to decipher the confusion of vocal or physical clues the teen leaves behind. But only teenagers knows for sure what they are feeling or what they are going to do, and they're not talking yet.

Other teenagers assert their freedom by trying to live a life of steady and quiet dignity. This means that they generally keep everything to themselves, leaving their parents as the last to know.

What is certain is that teenagers change their behavior when they first grope toward freedom, and your life is never quite the same again.

It starts when your teen begins to abandon safety and security. Parents' laps and arms, once taken for granted as stalwart and solid buttresses against an intimidating world, no longer draw the child toward the safety of their fortified grasp.

The security you provided as parents is replaced by the security of the herd. A herding instinct drives your young teen away from your immediate side. Teens and their friends wander farther and farther off, growing increasingly confident in their ability to navigate streets, malls, parking lots, book stores, and eateries without your help.

The strings attaching them to you aren't broken yet, for these younger teenagers still know that you are waiting for them. They can explore and roam without feeling constricted, embarrassed, or threatened, secure in the knowledge that there still is a parental safety net waiting to catch them if they fall.

Finally, though, your teen breaks the visual, verbal, and physical seams connecting the two of you. The break can be subtle. Or it can be abrupt. But it is probably final. One moment, your teenager is there by your side. The next moment...gone.

At some point in every teen's life, it is appropriate for us to allow this freedom (and to experience our own as well). So don't fight it. Your teenager is telling you that he or she has grown up and that "I don't need you anymore." Let it happen, putting on only as much leash as is necessary to make the passage as safe and uneventful as possible.

When is it appropriate to let go? That will depend on your teenager's personal style and maturity. Not all ten-year-olds are ready to leave their parents' sides willingly. Some strain at the hands to which others still cling nervously.

There are no hard-and-fast rules that will tell you when your teenager is ready. Don't compare your child to an older sibling or to your teenager's friends. Teens mature at their own rates, display their own styles and behaviors, and assert their freedom in different ways. Most instinctively set their own pace and somewhere along the way let their parents and other adults know what they are going to do. Alert parents sit back and observe how their individual teenagers handle the experience of freedom.

Freedom Is a Piece of Cake, Right?

As adults, most of us exercise freedom with an awareness that it is a combination of choice and responsibility. Most teenagers, unaccustomed to freedom, first have to learn that freedom involves any kind of conscious activity at all. Still, freedom does come eventually, and most teenagers adjust to it without too many major bumps in the road.

Be prepared to accept your teen's freedom, no matter how the process takes place. It doesn't always happen smoothly. My big day came when my son was ten.

He came home from school and announced that he was old enough to go to the comic book store without me. He would just ride his bike over and back again. We agreed that he should be back in one hour. It took only ten minutes to get there and ten minutes back. That left forty minutes to browse, buy, and take in the sights. No problem. A piece of cake. Those were his words, not mine.

It ended up taking three hours.

The story my teen gave differed somewhat from the official police version.

The police were most emphatic. "Your child got into this man's car. The man hoisted your son's bike into the back seat and gave your son a lift to the comic book store. The man waited while your son walked into the store to look around.

"It sure looked like this man and boy were loitering around the premises of a store and your son was casing the joint.

"So anyway, your son spent about a half an hour just looking around, picking up comics and reading them, and generally taking his time. The man went into the Super Quick next door and bought some coffee and pastries for himself and a soda for the kid."

I didn't say a thing. My son wasn't supposed to drink that sort of stuff. It did strange things to him. I just waited.

"After two hours, your child comes out loaded with comic books. He tells the man that he'll just take his bike now and walk it home. It isn't far. Well, the man didn't like this line of reasoning or something, 'cause he slammed the door in your son's face and took off real fast.

"Good thing we happened by just then, ma'am. A little young, isn't he, to be roaming the streets by himself? A good birching should do the trick, if you know what I mean. Sign here."

The police took my son's bike out of the cruiser and laid it on the grass. Then, they left.

My son said nothing throughout the whole story and didn't contradict the officer. After the police had left, he saw my face and spoke up quickly.

"It's like this," he began, as he walked over to his bike.

"I was almost there when my back tire blew." He kicked the rear wheel while I inspected it.

"Yes," I agreed, "it's flat."

"So," he continued, "I got off and started walking with it to the store. Well, you know that big field that used to be empty? It's not. Someone put a metal fence all around it so I had to walk on a busy street."

"*Westbelt?*" I screeched. "*That* busy street? You had to walk on *Westbelt*"?

"Don't get so upset," my son replied. "I'm here, aren't I? I'm in one piece. See?" He turned around. "There's no damage done.

"Anyway, I was walking my bike along the curb when this guy came up and stopped his car. He asked if I wanted a ride. I said no, 'cause I was all right. He didn't believe me, and said he'd follow me until I got to the store. I said okay, and I started walking my bike while this guy followed in his car. We finally got to the store and I was just locking my bike when this guy came over and said he would take me home. So, I said, 'Sure, if you're still here.'"

"And," I prompted him, "couldn't you have called me? There is a pay phone in front of the convenience store. In fact, there's two phones in front. Or you could have asked the proprietor if you could have used his phone. Isn't there a gas station about a hundred yards further down? You could have gotten the gas station attendant to pump your tire."

My son gave me his superior look. *Mothers! What do they know!*

He continued. "Well, I kept stalling. I looked at the comics I wanted. Then I bought them and went over to the Super Quick and played with the games over there. The guy wouldn't disappear. He was making me nervous. So, I stalled and got a soda and drank it, hoping he would go away. I didn't have any more money, and I had to leave. And that's when the officers saw me, just when the guy started putting my bike in the back of his car."

"Don't you believe me?"

Let's start over.

"It's not that I don't believe you," I started out slowly, "but there are..." and I saw his face.

I tried a different tactic.

"Couldn't you have called sooner? Couldn't you have told the Super Quick man or the comic book man that this man was pestering you?"

Again, I got that look, a cross between *Get real mom* and *You don't trust me?*

I tried one last time.

"Okay. Let me get this straight. You rode your bike until it got a flat in the rear tire. Next time, turn around and come home.

"Or, when you get to the store," and I emphasized my words, "*call me.* I won't ask what happened, but you must promise me that you'll call if something happens. Is it a deal?"

My son kicked the bike's rear wheel several times, gazed off into space for several moments, shoved his hands into his pockets, turned around and scanned my face, then said very slowly, "Oh, all right. If you insist. I could have taken care of myself, but I guess I can handle it your way."

"Oh," I added, "always carry change for the phone."

I knew from his withering look that I had overextended my parental concern and I walked back into the house.

Two hours later I received a phone call. It was my son. He had wheeled his bike over to the gas station to pump up his tire. There was no air pump. Could I come and get him now, please?

Preparing For Freedom

Freedom is the beginning of a teenager's independence from parents. It is going to happen, and it's not going to wait for you to give it your blessings. You have to prepare your child for freedom, then you have to trust your teen, whatever happens. You're not going to be there all the time. You'll be at work, at home, asleep. You must have faith that good sense will prevail, that your teen will handle freedom and its consequences without you. Make sure your teenager feels your trust and knows that you will be there if something goes wrong.

Expect your faith to be tested when your teenager first samples freedom. Being a teenager is tough, and it's especially tough emotionally. Give yourself and your teen some room. Think about what you are going to say to your teenager, and learn how to listen to what your teenager says in return. Communicate, making sure that each of you understands exactly what is being said by the other. Then stop looking over your teen's shoulder (or don't get caught if you do). This is not the time to doubt your teenager's words or ability to accomplish something without your help.

Make sure your teenager understands that things can go wrong—that busy streets, strange adults in strange cars, flat tires, and other unexpected surprises can cause unplanned disruptions and that ordinarily routine teenage activities like taking shortcuts, talking to strangers, and loitering in malls or convenience stores can become dangerous events. At the same time, don't make such a big deal that your teenager becomes inhibited, afraid to walk down the block or try a new bicycle route. You're walking on a tightrope. Communication and trust are the keys to maintaining your balance.

Again, there are no hard-and-fast rules. You need to judge how prepared your teen is to experience freedom. Some teenagers are always ready for a big adventure; others are more cautious. Parents need to listen to their teenager's feelings and fears and be supportive, not just when things go well but even more when they don't.

This is more than teaching your teen about freedom. A teenager is learning to exist in a teenage reality that often collides with an adult reality. Both parents and teenagers need to be able to communicate their fears and concerns to each other. The lines of the teenager-parent relationship are being redrawn. Make sure both of you are listening.

For example, suppose your teenager, like mine did, plans a solo trip he or she has never taken before. The two of you can go over the route beforehand and leave nothing to chance. Call attention to some of the directional landmarks. Banks, grocery stores, houses, all make great markers, especially if your teenager is not adept at the compass directions of North, South, East, and West.

Teens do have the habit of minimizing parents' words, so emphasize what is important for your teen to understand. If you have to explain the obvious, it may be that your teen is not quite ready to make the trip. Be explicit. Repeat the instructions as often as necessary until the teenager knows them by heart but not so stridently that your teen tunes you out in self-defense.

Give precise instructions about what to do if something goes wrong. Most of the time, these instructions will be to phone or come home right away. Make sure your teenager has a good idea about what to do when a situation he or she has never experienced before turns into a crisis.

Freedom's Consequences

Freedom is not always an easy concept for teenagers to grasp. For many, freedom is little more than a physical thing with no consequences in any realm other than the here-and-now. Teenagers may give no consideration to freedom's emotional or mental repercussions. They may also consider freedom to be an inalienable right to be defended vociferously whenever they perceive any kind of parental interference. Parents need to acknowledge teens' rights (inherent or otherwise) yet be ready to yank their teenagers back into the real world that their kids may not yet recognize.

Teenagers need to understand that freedom is not a private experience. It occurs in a social world and it can affect many other people. Teenagers often believe that their society is some sort of alternative universe, built around teenage perceptions and perspectives which differ from those of their parents. Parents may need to point out that actions have consequences in every universe. Freedom exists in a world of chain reactions.

Once my teenager came home from school and advised me that he and his friends were going to the mall—without supervision, without chaperoning, without any parental involvement whatsoever (except for limousine service).

"We want to be deposited at the mall to go to the book store and check out the chicks."

"Are we talking girls?" I asked.

"Yeah. Girls. I love it when they bend over and you can see down their sweaters."

"You know, they think the same kind of things about you. They love looking at your bottoms in those tight jeans."

My son was startled to learn that girls with whom he was friends were actually at the mall shopping for guys. The two groups met and promptly walked, talked, bought, and ate together. After I picked my son and his guy friends up, I overheard the following discussion in the back seat of the car.

"Did you see how much food she ate? I didn't know girls could eat so much. And talk. Boy, am I glad I'm not a girl. I thought those two were friends. Some friends! Did you hear what Nancy did to Mary Jane? She didn't like her making up to Stan so Nancy told Stan that Mary Jane still slept with all her teddy bears. Can you believe that?"

When we got home, my son thanked me for taking the guys and him to the mall. Then he said, "I thought that only girls gossiped."

"No," I answered. "Boys do it, too. It's part of freedom of speech." This opened the door for me to confront his teenage version of reality with my adult truths.

"Look, Hon, when you talk to your friends, I don't eavesdrop, but..."

"Yeah, well, it's all right. I didn't think."

"Hold it right there." I looked directly into his eyes and echoed his words. "You didn't think. The problem is that none of you think. It's really easy to pass along information, whether it is true or not, just as long as you don't get caught. It doesn't require any conscious effort."

He sighed a teenager's sigh. Then he looked far away. But I think he allowed himself to hear me, too.

"How would you like it if someone repeated a misstatement about you? Would you like all your friends to know?"

I paused. "What about Candy Simms? How would your friends react to that?"

This time I know he heard me.

"My friends! How dare you!"

"Your friends repeated stories in the mall which may or may not have been true."

"It is true!" my son yelled back. "I know it for a fact."

"Fine. Tell your friends what happened between you and Candy Simms and see if that is just as amusing."

My teen glared. Candy Simms was one girl that he wanted to stay away from, for life.

(In the sixth grade, Candy Simms had a crush on my teen, but my teen didn't like her. He ignored her and, even worse, spoke to other girls. As far as he was concerned, Candy Simms and he were just classmates. There was nothing more to it. Candy had a different idea.

(When the entire sixth grade went on a field trip, Candy and my teen rode the same bus. My son deliberately ignored Candy while talking to several other girls. Candy tried several times to join the group, but my teen didn't respond. In desperation, Candy exchanged seats with another kid and tried to get my teen's attention by talking loudly to him. When he still ignored her, Candy scratched his arm with her long red manicured nails. She then got up, approached the teacher and accused my teen of hitting her with his books.

(It was Candy Simms' word against his: girl against boy. He brought home a note explaining the incident. Word spread throughout the school and community that my teen fought with girls. He was labeled a troublemaker.)

"That's different." my teen replied.

"Oh really? Your reputation suffered because false 'factual' information got around without anyone bothering to learn the truth.

"The same is true of Mary Jane. It may be that Mary Jane still sleeps with all her teddy bears, but that's her business and no one else's. When you take a private confidence out into the open, people may get the wrong idea. I think that Nancy was jealous and wanted Stan for herself. She would say anything to discredit Mary Jane with Stan so that she could get her guy."

"Girls don't do that sort of thing," my son said.

"Well, what do boys do when they want the same thing? They fight? They start rumors? They smear the other guy to make him look particularly bad? Remember that there's always another side, another angle, that can explain a person's behavior. And, don't be so quick about making judgment calls. That incident with Candy Simms hurt you with the other girls' parents. They wanted to believe the worst of you."

"Yeah, well," and my teen yawned.

Freedom And Responsibility

Freedom brings surprises, even for adults. One of them is the realization that freedom is not really free. Like choices, freedom involves consequences. Many teenagers are not prepared when they are first introduced to this lesson. They want to believe that their freedom is equivalent to anarchy, that their behavior is insulated from the lives of others. In their individualized worlds, teenagers often act as if they are the centers of the universe and that their lives and actions have nothing to do with the lives of others.

My son, like his friends, didn't consider the consequences of his freedom—in the example above, his freedom to gossip. For him, the insinuations existed because they might be true. Who was he to defend or not to defend, to believe or not to believe what happened between the two girls and the boy? It made believable, captivating gossip—though my teen would never call it gossip—these "known" facts linked together by other, common, "known" facts.

Teens must understand that freedom has a price. As adults, we have learned that the price depends on the manner in which it is paid, the time when it is paid, where it is paid, and why it needs to be paid in the first place. Teenagers have to learn all these whys and wherefores. As parents, we need to teach our teenagers that responsibility goes along with action, regardless of who initiates the action in the first place. There is always a consequence, even when the teen is a reluctant participant.

Freedom is not an exemption from responsibility. It is taking on responsibility and learning how to live up to it. Teens don't always notice responsibilities. The ability to recognize and accept a responsibility is an acquired skill. But freedom makes the skill all the more important to learn. Left alone and nurtured properly, freedom is a teenager's passport to adult reality.

Sometimes, making sure our kids learn how to handle their freedom can be a struggle. It's not that we want to make our teens miserable or thwart their freedom, regardless of what they might say about our motives. But we have no choice except to embrace the struggle. Our teens must master the challenge of freedom before leaving home. It is the only way they will ever learn to be independent. Support and encourage your teens whenever possible. Otherwise, they'll never leave.

And you can imagine what *that* would mean.

CHAPTER 6

Communication

Communication is more than speaking. It includes listening, attention, and respect. It is not easy to communicate well. Communicating with someone you know, someone who may be communicating something using more than words alone, can be a challenge. Especially when the communication occurs between family members, it can be particularly difficult. Teens and parents often can't imagine how to get started or where to begin. It can be particularly painful for teens, many of whom feel intimidated, overwhelmed, or simply left in the dark.

Communication between parent and teen cannot be taken for granted. Teens do not always want to hear what their parents are saying. Sometimes teens literally refuse to hear. More often, they only pretend to hear or they only hear what they want to hear. After all, teens can easily convince themselves that their parents cannot understand what is going on in their lives. Only teens have a realistic perspective on their experiences-to-come. If circumstances don't work out the way their parents predicted, teens are likely to think, "I knew they didn't know what they were talking about." If the parent proves to be right, teens frequently resent that they "had to find out the hard way." Parents can't win.

Miscommunication is even easier when everyone speaks at the same time and refuses to hear what anyone else has to say. While your teen is trying to tell you one thing, you are trying to tell the kid something else. When you are not talking, you may be trying to think of what you are going to say next. After all, why listen? You already know you are right. Unfortunately, your teenager knows that he or she is right, too.

Once communication reaches this state of ineffectiveness, it affects all aspects of the parent/child relationship. Both you and your teen already "know" what the other is saying and what the other is going to say. You both "know" that you are not going to agree with what the other wants, so why listen at all? Communication breaks down, the teen proceeds with his or her plans, and you do likewise.

Don't Confuse Me with the Facts

Even when the message is important, parents and teens can find all sorts of reasons to ignore it. "It's like this," Franklin told me. "My parents told me I couldn't do this because it was wrong. I didn't want to believe them, even though I sort of knew they were telling me the truth. I had to prove I was right, so I went ahead and did it anyway. After I got in trouble, I kept hearing their words. But it was too late."

Teens especially let the stars blind them, even when the consequences are obvious to everyone else. Erica became so caught up in athletics at school that she couldn't hear her parents and her coach telling her to pay more attention to other parts of her life. The more she trained, the more completely she tuned out anything that challenged her teenage sense of purpose. "I wanted to win at any cost," Erica said. "It took me over. I became too involved with myself. No one could reach me. I turned off." It was obvious to everyone but her that something was wrong. Inside she was a knot of pain and turmoil. She stopped eating. She even ran away. She retreated into her own world and shut everyone else out. Finally, physical collapse brought reality to her attention. "Now I'm trapped," Erica sighed. "There's no one I can talk to or trust. I wish I had listened to my parents and coach the first time. I really blew it."

Lipping Off

Positive communication is too easily replaced by flip remarks and hurtful comments. Teens in particular cultivate the art of the unsubtle put-down. Sometimes parents are the victims; sometimes friends or strangers. But the result is the same in either case—an unnecessary, painful, and often destructive slap to the self-image.

Perhaps the behavior can be understood—teens are trying to differentiate themselves from parents and others, and they don't necessarily have the experience or the sophistication to understand the advantages of tact. Personal zingers are, in the teen's eye, an assertion of the power they think comes with maturity. But understanding is not approval. Smart-alec comments are not cute. They are not part of a phase your kid is going through. They are a sign that your teen still has some learning to do.

This kind of social behavior can become habitual, with potentially damaging results for your teen. One mother told me the hardly unusual example of her son. John had a loose tongue. He had a full arsenal of quips, one-liners, and put-downs, and he was more than willing to unload them on whoever he thought was in his way. It was cool to be cruel. John was a struggling salesman, mainly because he could not control his mouth. He spouted off to customers, to fellow employees, even to the owner of the store. Before long, he was spouting off to the unemployment counselor.

It's not just teenagers who use verbal karate. Parents can be just as guilty, with the same or even more damaging results. When the crossfire becomes so heated that mere words no longer seem able to express what either side wants to say, thoughtless tongues stick out to be counted. You might be able to understand or overlook a teen's hasty words. There is no excuse for a parent.

Consider what happened to George. He finally brought home a straight-A report card, and his parents kept a promise they had made by arranging for him to spend the summer in France. He put the tickets in a safe place and waited impatiently for school to end. A couple of days before his vacation was supposed to begin, George went to get his tickets. They were gone! He looked everywhere, with no luck. Then he reluctantly told his parents.

"What?" his father screamed. "That's impossible! You'd better look again; they must be in your room. But you'd better find them. No tickets, no trip. You hear me? No trip! I don't see how you can be so careless to lose them in the first place. What are you, some kind of jerk or something? You'd think that, if the trip was important to you, you'd take better care of your tickets."

George and his mother turned his room upside down. They moved the bed. They turned over the mattress and box springs. They looked under the loose floor boards. They took everything out of the desk and the bureau. They emptied the closet and looked in all the pockets of his clothes. They looked in his books and magazines. Nothing.

George's father marched into the room, hands on hips. "Of all the idiotic things to do. Losing your tickets two days before you're supposed to leave! Stupid, if you ask me. Do you know how much those tickets cost? You have no sense of money. I could talk until I'm blue in the face, and for what? You are sixteen. To think we were going to let you go all by yourself! I don't know who is stupider."

George sat on the edge of his bed. Maybe his father was right. Maybe he *was* just a doofus who would never be worthy of adulthood. His mother came over and, with a hug, said "You know, George, your Father loves you. But you disappointed him. He expected better of you. After all, you are our oldest." Some help! She left, and George sat there, feeling the volleyball in his throat and wondering if he would ever get over the vacation-that-might-have-been and the psychological beating he had just taken from both his parents. The tickets never did show up, and George spent many months coming to terms with the screw-up that even he acknowledged making.

Communicating With Teens

Teens do want to communicate. They lip off, in part, because they really are trying to reach out. Teens often resort to put-downs and zingers as a way of shouting "Listen to me! Pay attention to me! I'm important!" Unfortunately, teenagers are not always the most open with their lives and feelings. When they do seek out contact, parents need to make room to hear them. If their attempts are ignored or rebuffed, they may well go into a shell that makes communication impossible.

Or, they may turn to someone else. One doctor tells the sad story of his nephew. "He's a freshmen in college. He's only seventeen. He does all the wrong things. But that's not the half of it. He doesn't have anyone to talk to, at least not any adults. He doesn't trust his parents. He does confide in me sometimes, but what can I tell him? I listen, and it seems to help, but it's not like we're really talking. Most of the time, we're more like polite strangers. I don't really understand him, and I get the feeling that he is only telling me what he wants me to hear. How can I help someone when he can't or won't say what he means?"

I was blessed to have the confidence, not just of my teenager, but of many of his friends as well. My son even told his friends that I was there to listen without judging. Many of his buddies showed up on our doorstep—literally—to have real conversations with me. Why me and not their own parents? Because I listened, and their parents weren't always willing to.

Parents need to take the initiative. Talking a situation through is far better than letting it hang unresolved. Both teens and parents benefit from frequent heart-to-heart talks. Despite their apparent reluctance to talk, teens feel more comfortable sharing confidences, and parents feel more at ease hearing them. Teens might still keep a few secrets, but the best parent-teen relationships allow for open communications.

Teens need to know that you take them seriously. They need to know that you care and that you are giving them your time because you want to, not because you have to. They need to have someone who will listen without embarrassing them, criticizing them, or judging them. They need the assurance that you will be there when they want to talk and that you will not force your attention on them when they want to be quiet.

Teens are seldom obvious. Many teens would prefer that parents interpret their private thoughts and simply respond. Most parents are not mind-readers, however.

Teens often leave nebulous clues, if they leave any at all. Parents who know their teens and keep up with their teen's lives have an advantage. But even they have to remind their kids now and then that they do not have crystal balls.

Teens need you to recognize that they are saying something and to pay attention to what they are telling you, even if it sounds like nonsense. It's not nonsense to them. They need you to show, by listening, that you respect them as individuals with real lives. Ask questions whenever you have any uncertainty about what your teen is saying. Your questions reassure them that you are paying attention and that you really do want to understand what they are saying.

Communication also strengthens the parent-teen relationship. It keeps the avenues of dialogue open. If you expect your teen to come to you only when an emergency happens, your teen may never come to you, even in the middle of an emergency. Teens need to learn that they can confide in their parents without fear of pain, embarrassment, or confusion. They need to believe that their parents are fountains of information and guidance, not basins of indifference. Communication today opens the door to communication tomorrow.

Teens Really Do Hear

Joey was an excellent guitarist. He led his own band throughout high school. After he graduated, Joey decided that all he wanted to do was tour the country with his band. His parents were aghast. How could he think of such a thing? He needed a college education, and they were more than willing to pay for it.

Joey didn't agree. His parents were behind the times, he thought. He knew what he wanted out of life, and college wasn't very high on his list. His band felt the same way, so he left the college applications on his dresser and set out to make his fortune on the road.

For a while, things went well. The band developed a reputation that preceded them on a road that seemed to be paved with gold. His parents were proud of him, but they still wanted him to go to college. When Joey paid his folks a visit after about a year of musical success, they renewed their offer to send Joey to college or music school. Again, Joey said "No." He was making good money and having a great time. What more could he ask for? No, he'd keep on doing things his way.

But Joey's good fortune wasn't guaranteed. The band broke up. All his traveling had used up most of what he earned, so he didn't have much in the way of a nest egg. He moved to New England, tried to make it as a bar musician, learned how to make violins and guitars, and occasionally wrote home, mainly to ask for money. Three years later, he came home to stay. His first words to his parents were: "Is the offer to send me to college still open? I'd like to take you up on it now."

CHAPTER 7

Relationships

Relationships are important parts of every teenager's life. As far as my teen was concerned, all of his relationships, whether with his family or with the world in general, were Great Significant Moments.

Teen relationships evolve through two stages. During the first—call it the *pupal* stage, up to the age of fifteen or so—teens relate to others without much thought. They mean well, but they seldom think situations through. The success of their relationships is often just the luck of the draw. After the pupal stage, the *larval* stage continues throughout the rest of the teenage years. Here, teens struggle to make correct relationship choices. Then they stand back to see if they were right or wrong and to discover how well their choices reflect back on them. Older teens have learned through experience and discipline to make sounder judgments of others, and it shows.

Teens seldom follow straight lines through this evolution. Instead, they fluctuate and advance by fits and starts. One moment, they're calm, cool, and together. The next moment, they are baffled, confused, and disoriented about what's happening in a relationship, why it's happening, and what direction this new relationship may take them.

The Repeated Phrase Syndrome

Teens willingly communicate their feelings about their relationships. One device they use is the repetition of selected phrases. Teens revert to these "passive-aggressive" verbal zingers especially when they feel their relationship is threatened or insignificant. "Nobody loves me!...Leave me alone!...I know!...I can do it myself!...I can't wait to leave home!" are a few of the more familiar phrases. When teens use these phrases, they're often expressing feelings of inadequacy, guilt, betrayal, anger, or anguish. This is particularly common as teenagers mature and their relationships with parents (and everyone else) change. The old comfortable ways are coming to an end, and the family just doesn't quite seem the same.

Family Relationships

One of the hallmarks of their evolving relationships is that teens learn to recognize that their parents are only human. This is the beginning of the end. Parents no longer occupy the pedestal. Parents are no longer the only people in charge. They must learn to share their pedestal with the teenager, who is more than eager to occupy a place on it.

This transformation is part of the evolution of the teen. It reflects the teenager's conscious passage away from parental authority. The teenager is seeking a new identity in the eyes of the parent and a chance to establish him- or herself as an individual in school and the adult world. It can be an easy or a difficult transition, depending on how parents and teens conduct themselves through these times.

Teens become separatists as they realize—and you should, too—that they are no longer your property, if in fact they ever were. They belong to themselves. It's not a complete, instant reversal of awareness. It happens gradually. But the essence of the change is your teen's growing sense of individuality.

Teens don't always want your approval, nor do they want to hear about what you did before you became a parent. Teens don't want comparisons to anyone in the immediate or outside family. A particularly invidious comparison is to a sibling. For some teenagers, this "Sibling Trail" can be a path of thorns throughout their teenhood. Comparisons to older or younger siblings—even well-meant comparisons—can devastate a teenager's development as an autonomous individual.

One teenager described his experience of the Sibling Trail this way. This teen had a younger sibling whom he described as "perfect in every way." The younger teenager was brilliant in school and received all A's. The parents deferred to the younger sibling because this teen was "talented" in a parentally acceptable field (playing the piano as compared to being "just a writer"). The parents made no secret that the younger teen could go to Princeton or any other Ivy League school. The older teen, on the other hand, would have to go to a state school and make the best of it.

Many teens tell similar stories. They have had older or younger siblings who were good in school, made friends easily, or dated a lot. Sometimes, parents drew comparisons to pit one child against another. But whatever the reason (and none of these teens ever figured it out), the siblings were constantly stealing the limelight. To many, it seemed as if their parents never saw them. When their siblings finally moved out, the parents acted as if they noticed these teens for the very first time. *Well, looky here, we have another teenager. Where have you been all our lives?* As more than one teen has complained, "It's a little late in the day, don't you think, for them to notice us for the very first time? We actually existed for them. How nice!"

Parents can also unwittingly compare sons and daughters, usually to the disadvantage of the daughter. I have known a number of teenage girls whose brothers received cars at graduation—after all, they *were* boys and going to college out of town. But the same largesse was not extended to the girls who had also graduated and who were also going to school out of town. "Girls just don't need wheels." Several asked the rhetorical question, "Now, is that fair, or what?"

Understandably, teens do not like to be compared to siblings, other teens, or anyone else. They are not interested in how their siblings mastered a challenge or got through high school. "I've got all her teachers this year, and they won't let up. I'm me with my own ideas, not anyone else! Why can't they see that? Why can't they just leave me alone?"

Teens often realize that some of their siblings did make it possible for them to succeed. However, they still don't want Mom, Dad, or Mrs. Jacoby in Geometry class to remind them. "Just because Derbie got all A's doesn't mean that I'm going to get all A's. I do other things that Derbie didn't do. Just give me some credit for thinking on my own, will you?"

Family Outings

Teens have to believe they are autonomous, even when you and they know that they are still teenagers. Humor them whenever it is safe to do so.

Family togetherness is particularly fragile, at least in public. Teens frequently view going places with their families as one of the most difficult parts of the parent-teenager relationship. After all, they know (or are afraid) that teenagers who are seen with their parents, siblings, and other persons not of their peer group are just not socially acceptable. Listen for tip-off phrases like: "If I am seen with you, would you walk ahead of me?...If I am seen with you, would you walk behind me?...Please don't let anyone know that you're with me."

Being seen with you promises your teenager a horrible fate. Being noticed with parents, relatives, or siblings by other teens is too much for many teens to bear. The reactions of others tell us. Their pitying glances and small, understanding, tight smiles say it all. *What a loser!*

Certain rules have to be followed during outings with a teen. Get used to them. Shows of friendship or affection are not allowed. Holding your teen's hand or—Heaven forbid!—kissing your teen in public is absolutely unacceptable. Even speaking to your teen is pretty much taboo. Some other teen might actually see. You might do something with them on a weekday, but don't expect much cooperation during the weekend. Few teens want to give the impression that they have nothing to do during this prime teen time.

Expect to be challenged. Statements like: "Do I have to go shopping with you? Can't you just give me the money so I can go with a friend or something?" are quite in order. Your teen is likely to remind you, "I'm not a kid anymore." Get used to that last statement. Whether it is true or not, your teen believes it, and that is all that matters.

Many teens actually prefer to stay at home while the rest of the family goes out. One favorite excuse is, "I need to be here." For example, "I need to work on a project with Jim. He's got half of the material, and I can't finish the project without him. Besides, I can't reach him until later. He's out, and his parents don't know where he is. I guess that means I'm staying home, huh?"

Expect your teen to insist "I'm old enough!" It used to be a lot simpler to decide whether or not this was true. But today's news, movies, and tabloids ceaselessly remind us of the risks involved. Now, the decision is not so simple. At what age is it appropriate to leave a teenager home alone? This has to be your own personal decision. Even if you are not ready to give your teen this kind of responsibility, your teen will be the first, last, and always to tell you that he or she is ready, that things will get done while you are gone. Of course things will get done, but maybe not in the way you would have done them.

When you, your teen, and possibly the law finally agree on a suitable age for staying home alone, you should still take precautions to make sure that you, your teen, and your house all come out better for the experience. One of the best things you can do is to leave a *Home Alone Manual* which tells your teen everything you hope the teen will never need to know. Include at least the following information in your manual:

☞ *Names, numbers, and times* detailing where and when you can be reached. Make sure your teen understands how to use the phone to contact you if something comes up.

☞ *A best-friend list* including the full names, phone numbers, and present addresses of people your teen can contact in an emergency. Notify these friends and relatives whenever you are going out of town, and let them know that your teen may call them in case of an emergency or just to feel safer. Ask them to call and check with your teen now and then to make sure everything is okay. If they are really good friends, ask if they would have your teen over for dinner once or twice while you are gone.

☞ *Doctors and other emergency names and numbers*, including hospital names and addresses. Include a map and directions for getting to the doctor or the hospital. Make the directions as clear as possible. A lot of teenagers—possibly yours, as well—don't know east from west and, if they are like my teen, may consider asking for directions something worse than dying.

Some teens, like some adults, are not calm during an emergency. There are several steps you can take to make sure that your teen will be able to respond well to an emergency. Write down the 911 number, and have your teen practice what to say. Have a plan for getting to safety in case of a fire or similar disaster. Hold a fire drill and make sure your teen knows how to get out of the house or apartment. Point out the doors or windows to use, even attaching postees on the critical windows and doors. Make sure there is a ladder and a fire extinguisher available. Write the plan and directions out, and place a copy in the *Home Alone Manual.* Most teens won't view this kind of plan as an insulting commentary on their intelligence; they will recognize it as a back-up just in case something goes wrong. Make sure that your teen understands that everyone needs a safety net.

Your teen needs to understand the ground rules. For example, friends are not allowed in the house while you are gone and all regular house rules are to be obeyed. Let your teen know that if the house is too quiet for comfort, it is all right to go to a friend's house to sleep, as long as your teen calls and lets you know in person or by message where he or she is going to be for that night or weekend.

Finally, call the home when you arrive at your destination to let your teen know that everything is okay. You and your teen will be glad to know that the safety net is still there if it is needed.

Sooner or later, your teenager will learn how to cope on his or her own and you both will learn to trust his or her basic instincts. Before that happens, there may be moments when you return home to who-knows-what. Before you explode and condemn your teen to a lifetime of grounding, hear what he or she has to say. The sinkful of dishes may mean that the dishwasher broke down, and you really didn't expect your teen to get dishpan hands now, did you? Television trays are heavy, and it was much easier to let the food remain on the floor. Besides, you always told your teen to share his food, and that's what he was doing...with the dog. You should be happy instead of mad.

Relax. It is highly unlikely—though not impossible, I admit—that you will return home to find all the doors wide open and your teenager gone.

Everyday Teen Friendships

Teens have all kinds of friends. One is the *just-between-friends* friend. This is this teen's one and only genuine friend. No one else is quite so close. This friendship is tight. These teens do everything together. "Paul is a good guy, a regular guy. We just like to hang out together, that's all. We understand each other. He has other friends, but he prefers to be with me."

Another friend is the *confidential* friend. This is the friend your teen speaks to without hesitation. Your teen may confide everything to this and no other friend...or parent, for that matter. "I asked her to come over. We went downstairs so no one would listen. If I had wanted you to know, I would've spoken to you about it. Sometimes, you just can't help me."

Teenagers have many other friendships as well. My teen had friends who could solve his problems just by talking about them. He had indifferent friends who ignored his problems and others whom he could call on in a pinch. Finally, he had dead-beat friends who simply walked away from him, or vice versa, with no questions asked.

Teens change friendships often. You may never know whom your teen will bring home. Consider yourself fortunate to get to know the friend beyond the first casual greeting of "This is my Mom. This is so-and-so. We're going upstairs. See ya." And even if you get to know the friend, you may never be formally introduced to the friend's parent. That is pretty much unheard of. After all, who would want their parents to know their friend's parents? That would make things too easy for all the parents.

Sometimes my teen's casual-acquaintance friends simply appeared on the back doorstep. Once, one casual friend who lived three miles away biked over when he wanted to see my son about something. Somewhere en route his front tire blew. He walked his bent bike the remaining distance, the blown tire over his left shoulder, shivering all the way because it was cold and he wasn't wearing a jacket. By the time he arrived, my teen had already gone to work. So, I gave the casual friend an old sweater, drove him to work, and deposited his broken bike back at his house. (At least the friend, casual or not, had enough manners to keep apologizing for the trouble he was causing.)

Another type of "friend" is the one who remains "friends" with your teenager despite the fact that the teen hates your kid's guts. Why stay friends with someone you can't stomach? Maybe no one else but your teen tolerates the teen at all. A conversation with one of these can be enlightening.

"Your son sucks!"

"Beg your pardon?"

"You heard me. Your son sucks!"

"I must be missing something here. Could you be a little more specific?"

"You son thinks he's so great. Well, I'm here to tell you, he's not. What do you think about that?"

"I'm not sure. What exactly bothers you about my son?"

"Everything!"

"I'm sorry to hear that. He really is a great kid."

"Yeah, that's what my Mom used to say about me. Not anymore."

"Well, things happen."

"By the way, when is he going to be home? I need to talk to him about something."

I felt enlightened.

The old expression *you never know what the cat will drag in* describes teenage friendships perfectly. Your teen may pick up and collect strays from different and sordid places. From grade school and neighborhoods, Sunday and summer schools, camps, hobby and toy conventions, vacations, and libraries, friends can come like animals on migration through your home.

For many teens, friendships are transient matters of here-and-now. Friends today may be strangers tomorrow. That is the way of teen life. Teenagers often consider friends as kids to be dropped, picked up, or stuck to depending on the direction of the wind.

Parents and teens often disagree about the friends that teens should have. This, as you may have already learned, is one of the things which teens and parents skirmish over. Most of the time, the teen friendships that endure are the ones that should endure. But you never have the assurance before it is no longer needed. As parents, you need to stay one step ahead of your teen, if only to be there when friendships turn stormy, as they often do.

Be patient. Teenage friendships are like any other relationship—they need the constant work and tending

that your teen is learning to give them. Good teen friendships grow with trust, respect, and communication. As
your teen becomes a better judge of whom to trust, respect, and communicate with, you will begin to feel much
better about whom your teen chooses as friends.

The Opposite Sex

Teens maintain at least two types of opposite-sex friendships, *friend* friends and *date* friends. Friend friends play
a variety of roles, including soul searching, rambling for
hours on the phone, doing favors without emotional com-
plications, eating out or in, escorting to movies, dances, or
the mall, simple camaraderie, and general goofing around.
"She's a friend who happens to be a girl—and if it goes
into something else, I'll let you know. How's that?...I just
wanted to get him/her something special. We're not going
out. We're just friends."

Date friends are different. They are actual dates closer
to the traditional sense of the word. One teen gets picked
up, taken around, and kissed at the door, and the other
teen then drives home. In these modern days, it could be
the boy or the girl who does the driving. Many dates "go
dutch" or travel in groups, and many girls drive their own
cars. Sometimes you are involved, whether you want to be
or not. Many younger teens need to be chaperoned, or so
it seems to my old-fashioned sensibilities.

The things that go on during a date may seem a little
more free-wheeling than when we parents were dating,
but the results are often painfully familiar. When my teen
started dating at the age of twelve, I chaperoned his first
date. I did everything expected of me. I walked the mandatory football field behind the happy couple and sat four
rows away from them, pretending to be invisible while I

waited for the end of the movie and the obligatory food function of the date.

After the show, my son and his date climbed into the back seat while I put on my chauffeur's cap. In the back seat, my teen's hand slipped and slid around his date's shoulders and down her sides. He fondled a little and gave her one or two quick kisses, but all in all it was very sedate.

I sat a few tables away from the couple at *Hamburger A'Hoy*. When my teen got up to use the men's room, his date of three whole hours sidled over to my table, leaned forward, patted me on the shoulder, and asked if she could speak with me honestly. "Of course," I said. She told me that my teen didn't tongue-kiss well and that he didn't even try to make out, much less anything else. He was a dull date. Could she be driven home at once?

On another date, my teen took a young lady (a whole year younger, in fact) to the prom. She was a real knock-out in that tight, red leather dress. My teen never danced with her. He wasn't fast enough. She had just used him to get to the dance. He came home with a friend.

Not all dates end up like these, although some do. Sometimes, date friends even become friend friends (often with interesting results).

"Could you set up a picnic setting in the living room? Rebecca is bringing the tree." (The tree was a dead branch with construction paper green leaves tied to it.) "I told her to leave the bugs at home, unless they were fake."

"I thought you weren't dating Rebecca anymore."

"I'm not. This is just a friendly picnic."

"Oh."

Be aware, however, that affections probably move faster now than when you were a teenage dater. This doesn't mean that your teen or your teen's date will be any more crazed or uninhibited than you were. Sometimes (more often than you might suspect), both teens have been brought up to be responsible and thoughtful toward others. Nevertheless, the rules and expectations of dating have changed over the years. Give your teenager some personal rules to follow before he or she ventures into the real world of dating.

Whatever you feel about sex between teenagers, it happens. Both teenage boys and teenage girls need to know what is going on and how to keep the hormones, if not at bay, then at least under control. Boys and girls alike need to know the differences between lust, love, and respect. All teenagers should know the facts of life, especially in view of the dangers that intimacy can bring. *Just say no!* is an admirable ideal, but sometimes it is not enough.

Making contraceptives available to teenagers is a controversial subject, one that is heavily clouded by moral, religious, social, and practical concerns. Only you can make your own choice about this personal issue. For myself—and I regret it has come to this—I would like to see all boys carry a condom and know how to use it. Dads or close friends can show them how to put one on. (Don't do as I did, when my son was thirteen. I asked a pharmacist to give instructions.) All girls should also know what a condom is and how boys should use it. The risks just seem too great to leave it to chance.

I am not recommending that you encourage or ignore your teen's sexual activity. Abstinence *is* the best way to prevent a host of unwanted problems, such as pregnancy, AIDS, and the early, unplanned onset of adult responsibilities. But I also cannot encourage you to stick your head in the sand. Reality is not always what we want it to be, even if it ought to be. There are no easy answers. The issue is far more complex than asking teens to choose between restraint and anything-goes, and if we reduce the subject down to that choice, we are not going to be satisfied with the outcome very often. If it is any consolation, teenage sexual activity was a problem for our parents...and their parents as well. But the stakes seem to be getting higher with every decade. Make a decision you and your teen can live with.

Teachers And Teenagers

Teenagers also form relationships with their teachers. It stands to reason: teachers have your teens up to forty hours every week. Often classroom situations and environments dictate the terms of this relationship. Teachers establish rules and conditions that must be met by teenagers if they want to pass. Just as they do at home, teenagers sometimes fail to live up to those preconditions.

Often these relationships are adversarial. Teachers can seem like tyrants of arbitrary authority, especially to teenagers who are not always founts of open-mindedness and understanding to begin with. "You mean our grades are based on turning in our homework? Bummer!...Miss Polansky wants us to memorize all this by tomorrow. Doesn't she realize that I have other classes besides this one?...Mr. Lewis won't let me start another project until I finish this one. Some help he turned out to be!"

Teens often feel that teachers and schools are obstacles they have to struggle to overcome—often in futility. For many, the relationship is unrequited. Teachers and schools just don't care or listen. "They took him out of private school because he stopped working. Well, it wasn't his fault. He just couldn't talk to the teachers. How could he? The teachers just don't understand what he's saying. Then they report his activities to his parents. How gross!...The teachers just don't understand. Maybe they should try and see things his way for a change. It's not like he's being disruptive or something. You'd think they would try something different instead of just boring him to death."

Not all teens end up confronting their teachers and school, but many do. Pay attention to what your teen is telling you about school, even if it sounds like the same old and tired complaints. Pay attention to what schools and teachers are telling you about your teen. Schools are safe places for teens to learn how to deal with what they think is adversity. Far too many teens learn that the way to handle this kind of frustration is to drop out, to take it personally, or to blame their teachers or parents instead of taking responsibility themselves. It's much easier to step aside than it is to take any meaningful action.

Relationships with teenagers and teachers are constantly being redefined. It is difficult enough when teachers always seem to be saying "no" and restraining teenagers who want to be told "yes" and be given free reign. Teens need to realize that their teachers are not out to "get" them but are more concerned that the teens ultimately triumph in school and in society. Many teens have learned this untaught lesson of school, as my teen did when he left *Thank You* notes on his teachers' desks just before he graduated.

Just You And Me, Pal

Your relationship with your teenager will become more complicated as your teen matures. Throughout the teenage years, the challenge will be to balance your teen's urge to grow up with the equally strong and simultaneous urge to be catered to.

Don't expect miracles. Your teen means well, but slipping back into old, reliable, dependent ways is often a lot more comfortable. Comfortable, but not necessarily better. Encourage your teen to handle his or her own affairs—even if it means a blow-out between the two of you. Your teen will never learn if you are always standing there behind her or him.

You will be walking the high wire between the need to let your teen grow and the need to be there for your teen at the same time. Set a good example—teens learn by example. Be realistic. Teens will never be closer to perfect than the examples and role models they learn from. Stay willing to listen and to communicate. Keep your sense of humor; you're going to need it. Let the small incidents roll off your back and put your energy into the big ones. Keep the long run in mind, not what happened today when you (or your teen) lost your cool. It is the long run, after all, that makes the short run worthwhile.

CHAPTER 8

Testing the Waters

Teenagers discover the meaning of independence by testing the waters. It is heady stuff for most teens. They are groping to find the boundaries between their world and the outside world. This has to be a trial-and-error process. They are learning what it means to be adults, but they have no experience to guide them. The only time this exploration can cause problems is when teens cross over the line separating appropriate and inappropriate behavior. Alas, this happens more often than we'd like.

Testing is often conscious, but it is rarely well-planned behavior. Forget about extending a toe or two into the swimming pool or splashing cautiously into the foamy part of the surf. No! Teens more often than not plunge right in, giving little more than a thought to water temperature or hidden currents.

Testing is a means for teenagers to stretch themselves as far as they think they can without endangering their existing freedom. They are finding out exactly how far they can break the rules, policies, and dictates handed down by parents and other adults.

For teenagers, testing the waters is a way to find out what they can accomplish without too much trouble, risk, or harm. For parents, testing means "you're on permanent stand-by."

What Testing Means

At the wise old age of seventeen, my teen announced that he was a "free agent" and that I could not force him to do anything he didn't want to do. At five-eleven and one-sixty-five, he was absolutely right.

I *could* make his life very unhappy—miserable in fact. Extra chores, lights out by ten, no television (my teen just had to watch the news), no car, no phone calls (either incoming or outgoing), wash the kitchen, basement, and bathroom floors. *Don't play power games with me, toots.* But it wouldn't have made any permanent difference.

The little power we have over our teens wanes as they get older, bigger, stronger, and wiser. Nevertheless, as parents we are still responsible for helping our teenagers recognize where the boundary lines are drawn. The challenge is to do our jobs without getting caught up in our own egos or our own pictures of the way the world ought to work. Kids are going to test. Unless these tests concern matters of life and death, health, or money you don't have, let them have their victories, even when you know that they are not really victories and that they are going to rub them in anyway.

Keep your perspective. Little things like wearing new clothes to bed, reading adult magazines, staying up all night to study before a mid-term, sleeping on the floor, all are big steps to teenagers (and sometimes even bigger ones for their parents). The teenager is trying to break the shackles of youth and to put on the clothes of adulthood. Even if they are misguided, they are taking some of the first steps toward acting responsibly. We parents should try not to interfere unnecessarily.

When, Where, And How

Teenagers start testing the waters at no particular age.

"You'll know when," a condescending teenager once told me. "You can't help but notice," another one said.

It was my teen who set me straight: "It's to keep you on your toes, Mom. You don't want to fall asleep on the job, do you?"

There are no hard-and-fast rules about when testing begins or what form it will take. However, testing generally escalates through three forms. In the preteen years, say from ages nine to twelve, it usually resembles an *I-Dare-You* statement. Here, the teen may hear you, but be damned if she's going to answer, especially if it involves something she doesn't want to do. Is it time to eat? Time to take the garbage out? Time to wash the dog or clean the room? Your kid may see how long it will take for you to tear his earphones off or take away the remote for the television. It is a big game, one in which the teen sees how far he or she can go without jeopardizing your sympathy and patience.

From age twelve to age fifteen, or thereabouts, testing takes on its *Devil-May-Care* form. Instead of testing how far you will let yourself be pushed, the teen begins to explore how much the world will let itself be pushed. Teens are stretching themselves as far as they think they can without endangering their freedom. They are trying to find out how far they can break the rules, policies, and dictates of the adult world without getting into serious trouble, especially while they still remain semi-protected under our wings.

The last phase of testing is the *Look-Ma-No-Hands* phase. By this time, teens no longer think parents are needed to help them make decisions. During their early years, teens test to find out where the boundaries are. As they get older, teens try to make their own boundaries.

They will do things for themselves, because they think they know better than anyone else how to handle the situations. Most teens (and most parents) survive this phase, but getting through it can be a real adventure for both.

Rubber And Concrete Steps

Teenagers pass through these phases by taking both rubber and concrete steps. *Rubber* steps are the inconsequential ones that allow the teenager to test the limits of personal power. These are the verbal potshots, one-liners, and wisecracks which have come to define the stereotype of teenage behavior. Teens can fall down taking rubber steps without any suffering (except, perhaps, for their pride). Let your teen take these steps. Rubber steps are practice steps which are harmless to everything (except, perhaps, your pride or your sense of order).

Concrete steps are much more significant. These have the potential of hurting your teenagers more, but they also offer the greatest and most meaningful rewards. Concrete steps are the ones teenagers take when they think they're ready for an expansion of their lives. Teenagers take concrete steps to alert their parents that the older, established order is due for a change.

The change will come, and when it does, it can be rough on everyone. For your teenager, it becomes the basis of further muscle-flexing. For parents, it becomes an invitation to controversy and shouting matches.

When this happens to you, remember that your teen is trying to tell you something. Listen to your kids. Don't feel threatened by the new or fresh ideas they are expressing. Your teens are explaining themselves to you. Don't dismiss them out of hand or back them into a corner without trying see life through the window they are opening for you.

One-Liners

One-liners are thoughts that come out of your teen's mouths needlessly and spontaneously. They are trying to express themselves conclusively, so they may use words and phrases rich in shock value. Don't be surprised when your teen says something like: "You can't order me around!...I'm old enough!...Stay away from me!...You can't mean it!...I don't have to listen to this crap!...You'll be sorry!...I'm taller, heavier, stronger, and smarter, so..there!...Don't touch!...I can do that if I want to!...Don't force me!"

One-liners are some of the tools of testing. Once they are said, they cannot be taken back. They are now parts of the parents' domain. Teens use one-liners to speak their minds without parental censorship, to express themselves as semi-independent pre-adults. They are trying to prove to their parents (and to themselves) that they are in control of their lives. To prove that control, they have to test. And they have to win the test without getting into too much trouble.

Parents need to understand this and not allow these one-liners to color their thoughts or actions. It is too easy to assume that the teen is simply defying and to slam a foot down lest this behavior continue. And, on the surface, your instincts would be right. But parents need to recognize that one-liners are smaller parts of the larger world of testing. Teens will forever be testing, and they have to if they are to grow to adulthood.

First Plunges

When teenagers first take the plunge, they are sending you the message that they are starting to grow up. This is their time to experiment. They want to confront the reality you have created for them. And they can't lose. They are still within your protective environment.

No one gets hurt permanently in the process, but there will be some pain involved, probably on both sides. As parents, we should understand this process. Didn't *we* try breaking the rules when we were teenagers? Didn't *we* deliver one-line blasts at our parents, too? Didn't *we* use planned strategies as parts of our routines?

Strategy

Strategy? Of course! Multifaceted ones. Testing may not be planned in advance, but it does involve a certain amount of intention. The first facet involves dancing around an established rule, knowingly violating some procedure or understanding that you have agreed on for years. This is done consciously and perhaps underhandedly. Your teen knows that testing works better when only one parent is present. (He or she may even set it up by getting one parent out of the way or waiting until one parent is not present.)

The second is pure emotional exploitation. Your teen offers confrontational statements, heavy soliloquies, and shovels-full of teenage logic. You, the parent, had no idea what your teen wants until now. Your teen is counting on your parental explosion. The principle here is simple. Parents don't think clearly when bedeviled. We say things that shouldn't be said. We give ultimatums. We try and bluff back. We act out of fear. We respond out of distrust. We become frustrated. Then we cave in. We are not ourselves until much later when we are trying to explain the teen's victory to our spouse.

Finally comes the self-congratulations when teens realize that they've won. They've gotten what they've wanted, and now they can rest comfortably with their

newly forged freedom. But, can they? While they exchange high-fives and pat each other on the back, we
parents wonder if our teenagers really understand the
consequences with which they will now have to live. Our
secret strategy may well be to let them win so they can
experience first-hand what adult boundaries really mean.

If you feel that your teens are trying to disrupt your
life, you're right. They are. It is part of their experimentation with life on a miniature scale...like miniature golf.
It's not the real thing. It's the teens' way of finishing all
eighteen holes. On the miniature golf course of teenage
life, parents are the rough equivalents of clowns and
windmills.

Points Of View

Teenagers have their own points of view, and these provide all the justification they need to pursue their testing.
When my teen was around twelve, he started educating
me about his. It was electrifying for him, this intellectual
repartee. The ground rules for our emerging relationship
were still taking shape. Misunderstandings could produce
tortuous results. I had to learn to identify the points of
view that justified in his mind the testing of the waters.
At least they made sense to him.

- Words no longer had absolute meanings. They meant
  what he meant them to mean. Only the point of view had
  an absolute meaning to this budding Plato.
- We were engaged in a form of combat. Whenever he col-
  lected a new piece of freedom, got his way, or extended
  his splash zone, he got the best of me. His victories were
  final. Mine were only temporary.
- He could throw caution to the wind. He could make his
  poor judgments. He could rush into any situation without
  thinking. He didn't have to discuss his plans beforehand,

if he even made them. He could forget existing rules if
they didn't serve his purpose. Mom would have to catch
him if he fell...but he wasn't going to fall.

☞ Rules would stretch to accommodate him. Mom would let
him get away with it this time. And after this time, then
every time, because he had proven that he didn't need
the rule any more.

☞ He really didn't mean for it to happen. It just did!

Warning Flags

Alert parents will keep their attention on the horizon and
not be distracted by the testings of the moment. Most of
these will be insignificant and not worth wasting time on
them. On the other hand, some testing triggers warning
signals that need to be heeded. For me, these situations
included:

☞ Any situation that required my permission, including
transportation, hotel reservations, and money.

☞ Catalogue-purchases of things like survival guides, mili-
tary literature (material from bomb building to acquiring
semi-automatic weapons), museum replicas (battle-ready
swords, daggers, axes, shields, helmets), and other material my teen knew I didn't approve of.

☞ Videos of all types—Japanese-language, heavy metal car-
toons and the like. I always suspected that my teen was
trying to find out how much misery and intellectual violation he had to inflict before I became a zombie and sub-
mitted to his will altogether.

☞ Anything involving naked anything.

Handling Testing

Coping with testing without losing your cool is not easy.
It takes strength and resilience to keep teenagers on the
pavement while allowing them their necessary freedom. I
had to learn the hard way.

Testing And Rules: The Comic Book Convention My teen enjoyed comic book conventions. They usually started around nine in the morning and lasted until well past midnight. These events also highlighted his dislike of clocks and telephones. Watches were annoyances and phones just didn't exist.

One day I chauffeured my teen and a friend to a comic book convention at a nearby hotel. Before they got out of the car, he promised to call me when they were ready to be picked up. This was at eight in the morning.

At six that evening, I was still waiting for the promised phone call.

At eight, I called the hotel and asked to page my son. They didn't page at comic book conventions, but the receptionist put me in touch with one of the convention sponsors, who told me not to worry. Did anybody in particular know my teen? I gave them a few names. The adult in charge told me that he would pass on my message.

At half past nine, I drove to the hotel. The convention room itself was almost empty. No one had seen my son or his friend in quite some time. I tried all the other rooms: the role-playing workshop, the film screening, the food concessions. No one had seen him. My teen didn't exist. I was getting desperate.

Finally, at ten o'clock, I was paged. I ran to the nearest phone in the lobby. It was my lost teen.

His friend's father had picked them up and taken them out to eat. The friend's father couldn't imagine why I wasn't home waiting for my son!

What could I do, now that I had been handed this act of independence on a platter of thoughtlessness? Perhaps my son was ready to take the next step toward adulthood, but the step he had just taken wasn't it. I started by reminding myself who was in charge. It was *not* my teen-ager.

I refused to overreact. No shouting, punishing, issuing dire threats or warnings. Lecturing my teen wouldn't have done any good—he'd just turn off and stop listening. The last thing a teen wants is to be scolded in front of a friend or, worse yet, in front of a friend's parents. This would accomplish nothing and he would not have gained any-thing from the experience (except perhaps for a little sophistication in testing skills). This would have been unsatisfactory. There were lessons to be learned from this.

I counted to ten. I told my son I had been worried about him and that I was glad everything was all right. I spoke with his friend's father, with whom I could carry on a calm and less emotional discussion.

We returned home. Before I banished him to his room, I reminded him that we had an agreement about what the rules were. I had given permission for the comic show, not a post-convention party about which I had no information. The next time plans change, call home. If you don't call next time, you'd better come right home. And even if it is okay to stay out later, you will still have to be home by a certain time. You just don't go around changing the rules unilaterally, especially when everyone else thinks the old rules are still in effect.

Part of testing limits is learning to recognize that there are consequences to crossing lines. For a week after he returned from the comic convention, my teen was not allowed to listen to his music tapes. I made sure that the severity of the punishment did not exceed the severity of the crime (thought he might not have agreed). I was not out for vengeance, but it was important to impress on my son that testing could only be taken so far before his hand got slapped.

Testing And Failure: The Model United Nations When he was in high school, my son went on a school-sanctioned trip to a Model United Nations day at a college located about three hours away. The event was going to last all day. My teen told me that he would be back at nine that evening. Would I please pick him up in the school's front parking lot?

Well after two in the morning, I was still waiting for my teen to return.

Instead of riding home in the school bus, my teen decided to ride back in a friend's car. Somewhere between Akron and Cleveland, he and his friend took a wrong turn. They stopped for dinner. They asked for directions. They asked for directions again. They consulted a map several times. They got lost on some country road that meandered in the general direction of Pennsylvania.

What went wrong? My teen and his friend took a concrete step to show that they were grown up enough. They meant well. But their testing failed. Their reasoning and deductions weren't quite sharp enough to get them out of trouble. Perhaps they should have known what to do, but they got frazzled and didn't think.

What should they have done? They could have started by calling home and letting us know that the plans had changed. He and his friend should have planned their route home and gone over it with a teacher or other adult before they left the college. They could even have asked a teacher or other adult who knew the route to travel with them. And, once it was obvious that they would be late, they should have called home to let us know.

To test and fail is not easy for teens to accept. To call home or ask for help would have been to admit failure and to acknowledge that maybe they weren't quite as grown-up as they wanted us to think they were. In many ways, testing is a teenager's way of maintaining the fiction that they are not really teenagers. Our dilemma is this: they *are* teenagers. We don't want to break their spirit or deflate their self-images, but we can't let them grope their ways into adulthood thinking that they'll never have to say, "Oops, I goofed."

Testing And Responsibility: Phone Calls When I felt he was old enough, I put a phone in my teen's room. A little later, he found a long-distance girlfriend. They wrote. They called. They even spent three summer days together to firm up their relationship.

Two weeks later, it didn't matter. She dumped him. The phone bill suffered almost as much as my teen. Four hundred dollars each month for three months. Long calls to his ex-girlfriend for many late night hours. Between two and four AM.

Why? "It seemed like a good idea at the time. It took me a couple of tries to get through, and, when she hung up on me, I had to redial to finish the conversation. It took me several tries to finish a conversation with her, you know?"

"Yes, I know. But, did you ever stop and think how much money you would've saved by not making those phone calls?"

I had made the rules very clear when I put in the phone. He was responsible for all phone charges except for the basic fees. He paid every penny of these long distance charges. And the girl still didn't come back.

It's hard for a teenager to test, fail, and take responsibility for the consequences. But it is an essential lesson of growing up. Teens have to learn that becoming an adult is not always as smooth and automatic a process as they might wish.

The transition is easier if your teen understands what the rules are. In the case of my son, there was only one basic rule: he had to pay for all his long distance phone calls. If his allowance didn't cover the bill, he could do extra chores around the house in addition to his regular teen tasks. As long as he followed this one rule, he could keep his phone. The point was that he needed to learn discretion and restraint and to take responsibility for the results of his testing.

Let The Testing Begin!

It's a teenager's nature to test, starting at any age between nine and nineteen. Parents need to be prepared for the transition, consistent in defining the rules, and persistent in responding to their teenager's challenges.

Teens must learn how to live in an adult world. It's a parent's lot to accept testing as a fact of life. Testing requires that the parent exercise the responsibility and maturity that the teenager is working toward. Testing is one way teenagers learn this lesson.

How do you know when the time has come to reward the testing and give your teen a little more room? *You'll know when*...remember? Pay attention to the way your teen handles testing and its consequences. Once your teen shows consistent and responsible testing behavior, the time has arrived. Your own relationship with your kids will change, as well—finally, both you and your teen will be in agreement.

However, your teen must learn that testing deeper water involves more choices and increased responsibilities. Your teen must be held liable for both. Teens must follow their actions through whether they want to or not.

There is no free ride, except for the very young, not for the parents and certainly not for the teenager.

CHAPTER 9

Manipulation

They don't just start when they enter the teen years. And they continue long after they graduate to adulthood. But during their teenage years, teens hone their manipulating skills to a fine edge.

Manipulation is the teen's ability to manage or control the parent (or anyone else, for that matter). It works in large measure because most parents love their kids and take their responsibilities seriously. Teenagers may manipulate consciously or unconsciously. The acid test of manipulation is how well the teenager is able to distract, redirect, influence or control the parent. Manipulation can occur at any given time or in any given event, my teenager once told me. It serves the purpose of getting what the teen wants, another teen admitted openly. As far as teens are concerned, the teen years are open season for manipulation, and they don't even need licenses.

Not all manipulation is harmful. It is usually not even premeditated. Most of it is natural and benign. Manipulation is just another part of the teenager's experience of growing up. It is parents who often get rolled, simply because parents, in the eyes of the teenager, are deserving victims. They have what the teenager wants, and that fact is the fundamental justification for manipulation. But anyone—parent, friend, teacher, stranger—is fair game.

Some teenagers manipulate quite well. Some—though not many—don't even try to take their parents for the song and dance. Between the extremes are found most teenagers, for whom manipulation in one form or several is totally normal.

Whittling Parents Down

Manipulation is limited only by the imagination of the teenager, but it often follows certain patterns. Frequently, it is little more than a persistent, non-subtle effort to get the parent to give up the fight. It is an invitation to play an endurance game that the teenager is confident of winning. Most of the time, teens play this game for relatively minor stakes. But that doesn't make it any less annoying.

My son's first obvious attempt to whittle me down involved "girlie magazines." For a while during his early teenage years, he was unusually willing to accompany me to the grocery store. "Why should this be," I thought, "when in most other respects he wouldn't be caught dead with me?"

The reason was, it turned out, that he enjoyed the magazine stand, which the store manager, no doubt as a public service to this progressive-minded town, kept stocked with *Playboy, Penthouse,* and several of their less-mainstream competitors. As soon as I would offer to buy one for him, he would casually put the magazine back into its rack, stare off into space, and say, "No, it's nothing. I just wanted to read the story about that Ethiopian poet. You know, this magazine has some pretty good articles."

I didn't really buy the bridge, but I was more than a little uncomfortable. The troglodyte store manager had placed his magazine racks in the front of the store, where anyone shopping for milk, antacids, or disposable diapers could see my son salivating over the promise of intellectual growth. My son knew that I was vulnerable and that, if he just persisted, I would become weary of the embarrassing fight over his reading habits.

The Passion Play

Manipulation is also a psychological weapon. For most parents, there is no defense against an assault of a guilt commando. Teens know that the appeal to guilt works best when it comes as a surprise attack. Parents, caught unaware, are forced to make snap judgments. Teens are very aware that parents facing an immediate decision are likely to give them what they want, especially when their parents' actions promises to affect the teens' well-being.

Sometimes, the sob story is pretty transparent. Head in hands, tragedy oozing out of every pore, your teen wails, "You are killing me. Just wait. You'll be sorry when I'm not around anymore!" Then the teen sighs, stops breathing, and throws himself or herself on the couch, chair, stairs, or any other roughly horizontal place.

At other times, the story is much more sophisticated. "I needed to get to the library before it closed. It's your fault I can't make it, because you didn't come home sooner. What am I supposed to tell my teacher? That I'm flunking tenth grade because you came home too late to take me to the library?"

It is hard to argue with logic like that, especially when you are preoccupied with your own concerns. Teens depend on your reluctance to stand there and argue with them. The scenario is transparent. Your teen wants you to accept the blame for the situation and to take on the responsibility for clearing the problem up. It wasn't you who didn't get to the library on your own initiative or finish your homework on time. But *what if...?* Maybe you *did* come home late...maybe you *did* let your kid down...maybe your teen *is* failing tenth grade. So the feeling that you have no choice but to give in and take the kid to the library is totally normal...and predictable. Your teen counts on it.

Playing On Your Sympathy

Sympathy is a powerful emotion, one that teenagers quickly learn can be manipulated. A long face, an anguished look, a hang-dog expression, a believable *woe is me!* attitude, all can touch nerves that are insensitive to mere words. Sympathy is one of the first emotional states that kids learn to recognize. A quality that makes small children feel good, sympathy is a weakness that teenagers exploit.

"Mom! I need the car!"

"You're grounded from using the car this week. Remember the gasoline tank you forgot to fill? Remember who had to walk the five miles to the nearest gas station?"

"I haven't forgotten. But, mom, this is important! You don't want me to fail...do you?"

"Fail? Fail what? Look, I let you have the car this morning to go the library. Be grateful that I didn't make you walk the mile and a half to work."

"This is different, mom. I promise I'll be more careful this time if you will only let me use the car...just this once...please!"

Your resolve crumbles in the face of this melancholy plea. You give in. Your kid drives off on the mysterious errand. Probably using your keys, too.

The Fait Accompli

One of your teen's manipulation purposes can be to set you up, to put you in a position where you can do nothing to undo the results of the manipulation. You realize soon enough that you've been had, but there isn't anything you can do about it. You open the door, and the kid takes over. Your teen gets what he or she wanted. He or she redirects your instructions, maneuvers you into not enforcing your words, and wraps you around his or her finger. All you can do is sit and fume and tell yourself that this is the last time you're going to be suckered like this.

"Mom...I've got to make a call. I'll only be on the phone for a few minutes. No more than that. I promise."

You want to believe your teen. After all, he or she has just asked you for your trust. "Okay, but I have some calls I need to make before five."

Twenty minutes later, your teen is still on the phone. You saunter over and find out that she's talking to Phyllis. "Didn't you just speak to her two hours ago? What is so important that you have to speak to her again?"

With a remorseful look, your teen says, "I've got to. I forgot to tell her something important."

So you deliver another ultimatum and walk away, confident that your teen will finish up the conversation soon. A half hour later, you return. Your still-jabbering teen smiles, waves, and you walk away again. *Just wait until your father (mother) gets home!*

Divide And Conquer

Teens have known for a long time that they have two parents. All the books on parenting insist that both parents need to present a unified front when dealing with their children. Even young kids know enough to ask Daddy when Mommy says "No." Kids who can play one parent against the other successfully are in control of the relationship. Parents and other experts know this well. Why, then, do so many parents act as if this were news?

Mary and her mother Lorraine had been working on a crisis for some time. Early on, they quarreled over the curfew that Lorraine insisted on. At first, they worked out a compromise that satisfied both of them. But the peace didn't last. As Mary grew older, curfew became one of many things that came between them. Mary started cutting classes; she didn't do her homework; she smoked and drank.

Lorraine didn't get much help from Clete, her former husband and Mary's father. When Clete picked Mary up for the weekends and holidays, he generally took her side. Mary counted on his support and used it to thumb her nose at Lorraine whenever the two of them argued. Lorraine shrugged her shoulders and wondered what Clete let Mary do when she was staying with him.

One day, the guidance counselor at school called. "Where is Mary today?" he asked. Obviously, not at school. When Mary came home, she and Lorraine had it out. "If you can't behave, I'll make arrangements for you to live at your father's." The magic word! *Father's.*

Mary left to live with Clete. It lasted about two weeks, until Mary moved out with the intention of living on the street. A truant officer brought her home. Lorraine cracked the whip. No smoking in the house. No alcohol. Mandatory school. Mary rebelled, and once again, Clete got a phone call. Mary packed up, promising to stay with her father from now on. It lasted a month this time.

This pattern went on for more than a year. Whenever life with Lorraine became uncomfortable, Mary manipulated Lorraine into a blow-out fight that ended with Mary's leaving to live with Clete. A month or so later,

Mary would return until the next time she felt a teenager's cabin fever. Clete's place became a refuge. Mary knew that her mother would give in and send her to live with her father, and she was more than willing to take advantage of the fact.

Until Clete wised up. He finally recognized what was going on. When the phone call came from Lorraine one more time, he made arrangements for Mary to attend the state school for minors until she graduated, the equivalent of an orphanage and juvenile hall in one building. Suddenly, living with Mom didn't seem so bad. Mary returned to Lorraine, this time to stay. And she did graduate. The fights and disagreements with Lorraine never really stopped, but Clete and Lorraine were finally able to speak with a single voice.

Relatives

If your teen can manipulate you, he or she can absolutely snow a relative and recruit an ally in the process. Teens recognize that *relative* is another word for *patsy*. Relatives love without responsibility. They give without misgivings. They are family, which gives them the right to spoil without having to live with the consequences. Relatives might just as well come equipped with a teen-sized handle conveniently attached.

"Don't you have some homework to do?" you ask your teen, who has just camped out on your living room floor with a pile of comic books, a plate full of his Aunt's chocolate chip cookies, and a quart of milk.

"Oh, he's all right. Leave him alone," says your sister-in-law. "When we come to visit, we want it to be a holiday. Don't make him do something he doesn't want to."

You look at your teenager. He grins back at you. You look at your sister-in-law. She grins, too.

Picking Fights

Your teen may have already learned that the mere threat of a confrontation can be a powerful weapon. You don't want to wave the acrimony flag in public, and your kid knows it. The thought of an embarrassing quarrel for the whole world to watch—at least that is the way it seems—is a powerful inducement for you to give in. Public venues are ideal staging grounds. Bookstores, restaurants, clothing stores, for example, are usually quiet enough so your argument will disrupt the peace and crowded enough that it will attract lots of attention.

The best time to stage a planned argument, however, is in front of doting relatives. Your teen starts to whine or complain. You want to quell the fire, but you know that negotiation will be futile. So, you respond like a dictator. "Be quiet!...Not here!...Not now!...I'm not going to discuss it!...Shut up and stop causing a scene!" Your relatives, aghast at this wanton display of your immaturity, slip their arms around your teen, pull the innocent child away, and give your teen whatever your teen set out to get in the first place.

Procrastination

Procrastination is an inverted form of manipulation. It is a teen's way of *not* doing what the teen doesn't want to do. Everyone procrastinates. But teens have not always learned enough about consequences to get the distasteful over with. Teens often live in the immediate moment. Understanding that something will hang over their heads as long as it remains undone does not always come naturally.

Teens often rationalize their procrastination. "I'll do it later when I can think clearly...It doesn't have to be done right now...It's not that important...It can wait."

These are typical responses. Sometimes, they even sound persuasive. After all, most parents want to believe that their kids are responsible, that they will do what they need to do at their own paces, even if it does take a little longer. "Trust me!" your teen says.

And you want to trust. Sometimes your trust is well-placed. Your teen wakes up one morning, sees the sunlight streaming through the window, and realizes it is time to get up. Sometimes, however, your teen rolls over, pulls down the blinds, and goes back to sleep. More often, your teen resets the alarm clock and gets up later, when there isn't time to do everything. Not enough gets done, or else it gets done too late to make any difference.

Evasion

A variation on procrastination is evasion. Teens learn that successful manipulation can be a matter of not saying and not doing. An evasion is a slippery way of getting around something that is distasteful or uncomfortable. Evasion is often passive, instead of active, tactical instead of strategic, and an effective method for getting a parent off a teen's back. It works particularly well when only one parent is present and when the teenager has something that the parent wants.

Such as information. Sometimes, teens are in a hurry and don't have time to tell you everything you want to know. Sometimes, they feel that your questions invade their privacy. Sometimes, they simply enjoy the power that evasion gives them over you. A typical evasion might go something like the following:

"Hello, Mr. Bloom. I'm Ted. I'm here to pick up Jenny."

"Nice to meet you, Ted. Before you go, there are a couple of things I'd like to know. Where are you going?

When are you going to be back? How are you getting there? You know, stuff like that."

"Sure, Mr. Bloom. By the way, I come highly recommended. Jenny knows me through school and, uh, my teachers can vouch for me. You can call my parents if you have any questions. Oh, hi, Jenny. Let's split. See ya later, Mr. Bloom."

Mr. Bloom did his best to find out what he wanted to know. But despite his efforts, he remained in the dark. He had been outmaneuvered, in part because he underestimated Ted and Jenny. He expected that all he had to do was to ask for the information, and Ted did nothing to disabuse him of the notion...until he and Jenny "split" and Mr. Bloom spent the evening wondering if Ted had been hiding something. Mr. Bloom would have been much more successful if he had recognized that Ted was a teenager and had Ted write down the details. (If this happens to you, have paper and pencil handy. Otherwise the information may show up in strange places—toilet paper works well, I hear.)

Dealing With Normal Manipulation

Manipulation may be a normal part of teenage behavior, but it doesn't have to become the central theme of your family life. You are the primary influence in how often your teenager resorts to manipulation. You are the parent, and only you can make sure that the manipulation game is played by the rules. You may never prevent your teen (or anyone else) from manipulating, but there are steps you can take to keep manipulation from getting out of hand.

First, accept that manipulation is a fact of life. It is going to occur. You are going to be manipulated. So stay aware. If you are to be conned, then be conned knowingly.

Don't go through your son's or daughter's teenage years with a *my-little-darling-would-never-do-anything-like-that!* attitude. That only reinforces the manipulation habit, making it much more ingrained and difficult to stem.

Manipulation begins as a test, a teen's empirical experiment in cause and effect. Teens test, then they sit back and wait to see what happens. If the test is successful, they do it again, not as a test this time, but as a learned behavior. If you are sensitive to your teen's early efforts at manipulation, you can redirect them into constructive or acceptable channels. Be alert to your teen's first efforts. Respond to them in a positive way. Your teen is only going to get more sophisticated, so stay alert.

Set a good example. You are your teen's most influential teacher, and your teen is going to do what he or she sees you do. If you manipulate your kids, they will manipulate you in return, using the same techniques they see you using. Don't take a teen's lack of intellectual sophistication for granted; teens are far more perceptive and impressionable than many parents believe.

Maintain realistic boundaries and keep them intact. Once you begin to compromise, you set in motion a domino effect. One thing leads to another when you get into the habit of overlooking manipulation. Before compromising parents know it, their teens learn how to take advantage of their parents' generosity. If you allow your teen to learn that manipulation is an appropriate, effective behavior whenever your teen feels like doing it, your teen will learn the lesson for life.

Make sure your teenager understands that there are no actions without consequences—no free lunches and no free rides. Manipulation is not done in a vacuum. Your teen will have to deal with the repercussions. They might not be earth-stopping consequences, but the teen's world will be affected even by what seems to be meaningless actions. There is always a next time that your teen will need to take into consideration.

Don't argue with your teen. Don't try to reason with your child, especially if he or she insists on twisting your words around. Simply define the rules and enforce them. Your teen really wants and needs direction and guidance; if you don't provide them, your child may well learn to manipulate instead of acting responsibly.

Don't bluff. Don't threaten. Don't lose your cool. Don't invite your teen to up the manipulation ante or call your bluff. If you say it, be prepared to do it. An empty threat is no threat at all. Your teen will learn very quickly if your threats are empty bluster. Don't threaten what you are not prepared to do and if you have to do it, then do it. Make it clear that manipulation is a game and discipline is not.

This doesn't mean you should be rigid. Teens have to feel that manipulation is *possible;* they have to be able to win now and then. Otherwise, their sense of autonomy and independence is threatened, and this opens the door to rebellion and unacceptable behavior. Once you have been manipulated so far, draw the line. Let your teen know that the manipulation has gone as far as it is going to go. You have bought into the shenanigans up to now, but the game is over. Be willing to say, "Just this once"; but also be prepared to say "No more."

Be an involved parent. Manipulation works much better when it is practiced on someone who is not aware of what is going on. Don't wait for the report card or the teacher's phone call to learn that your teen hasn't been finishing homework assignments, for example. By that time, habits of procrastination or manipulation may be well developed. Take the initiative to find out about your teen's activities. Call the teacher, for example, and ask how Sarah or Fred is doing.

Don't simply dismiss your teen's manipulation. Your teen may have some legitimate reasons for manipulating. There may be times, for example, when a teen manipulates or procrastinates because the consequences of proceeding ahead seem worse. The teen who is reluctant to go to school, for example, might simply be trying to get an unscheduled day of vacation. On the other hand, he or she may be afraid of the schoolyard bully or the class tease. Manipulation usually is done for a reason; as the parent, you need to find out what that reason is. If your teen is manipulating to solve a problem, you need to help your teen find a true solution. Always be ready to talk calmly. If you are so angry that you are losing control, walk away and cool off. You need to be able to communicate and compromise with a clear head.

Conditioned Manipulation

Most manipulation is relatively harmless, involving stakes like trips to the mall or using the car on Monday night. But even the most ordinary manipulation can become unacceptable if you fail to notice when it goes from a game to something more serious. One very real danger is that you and your teen will become conditioned to accept the manipulation and its consequences. Many teenagers have learned that all they need to do to control their parents is to get their parents to accept being manipulated. Manipulation escalates, and the inmates run the asylum. The teen assumes control, and both parent and teenager become conditioned to accept this state of affairs as comfortably normal.

Once this pattern is set, it is very difficult for parents to break it. Manipulation works. The more it works, the more it is used. And the more it is used, the more it becomes the normal state of affairs. When teenagers resort to manipulation on a routine basis, the fault almost always lies with the parent. To allow a teen over and over again to manipulate successfully is to send the message that "We are not interested. We don't want to be bothered. Go away." The teen hears, "Go ahead. Do what you want. We won't stand in the way."

At the age of sixteen, Georgeanne wanted some relief from her feuding parents, neither of whom wanted to parent and both of whom preferred being manipulated to confronting their daughter about her growing irresponsibility. She knew better than to flaunt them directly; she didn't have to. Indirect control was much more satisfying. She knew, for example, that her parents didn't approve of her gang friends. So she brought home a clean-shaven, well-dressed, well-spoken, employed, college-bound motorcycling young man. An exception to the generalization about motorcycle gang members? Hardly. He drank. He used drugs. He could not be depended on. Georgeanne never told her parents about these sides of his character, and her parents never looked beneath the surface. They were too willing to believe the appearances that their daughter had carefully orchestrated.

Georgeanne's parents had abdicated their responsibilities. Georgeanne knew they wouldn't stand up to her. All she had to do was raise her voice, tap her heels, start an argument, or threaten to do certain things, and her parents jumped. She was surprised to discover that not all adults were just as indulgent. She explained to me once, "I know what my boundaries are. My Mom and Dad...we have this agreement. My Mom lets me do what I want. My Dad buys me what I want. They both let me be responsible for myself. My parents are so much more accommodating than you are."

Unacceptable Manipulation

It doesn't happen often, but manipulation can escalate far enough to pose a physical threat to you, your teen, or someone else. Physical abuse results when manipulation becomes so desperate that it loses all semblance of decent social behavior. Rational restraints no longer suffice when a teen is willing to strike a parent or another person in order to get his or her way.

Teens who reach this point need help. Your first reaction may be to deny that there is a problem or that anything serious has happened. You may be tempted to ask what you did wrong or to theorize about the cause or causes of your teen's behavior. Perhaps you let your teen manipulate you for too long. Perhaps you backed your teenager into a relationship corner. Perhaps you let your kid get away with too much. Perhaps your child has discovered drugs. Perhaps there is something that your teen doesn't feel comfortable talking to you about. Perhaps it is none of these.

All this speculation can wait. If your relationship with your teen has reached this point, stop reading this book and get help. Consult a therapist, a social worker, or some other professional who can identify and address the real problem and take action if intervention is called for. Don't wait until you have to call the police to protect yourself from your child. Newspapers are far too full of stories about parents who failed to respond to warning signals.

There are no hard-and-fast rules for telling when manipulation is going too far. Only you, the parent, can determine when your teen's manipulative behavior is getting out of hand. Usually, it doesn't just happen. It builds over time and evolves a pattern of interaction in which give-and-take increasingly becomes give for the parent and take for the teen. You are the parent. If you do not take action to stop your teen from becoming a relationship bully, your teen may never learn to use appropriate social behavior.

Manipulation happens. All teens try it on for size at least once. Whether they try it again depends in part on you. As long as they are successful, teens will continue to manipulate, simultaneously testing the limits of manipulation and building confidence in their ability to manipulate you and others successfully. Manipulation is one way in which your teen explores the world. As a parent, you can make sure your teen learns that there are other methods of attaining goals which do not involve the ultimately futile effort to control the behavior of others.

CHAPTER 10

Privacy

Many teens share the same attitudes about their parents and their private lives: *Keep Out!...Enter At Your Own Risk!...No Exit!...No Admittance!...Stay Out!...This Means You!*

When teens share these attitudes, parents fear that their teenagers are trying to tell them something. And they are absolutely right. Teenagers *are* trying to tell us something. Teens are telling us that it's time for parents to give them some room, some space, so that they can get on with the business of living within their own parameters without too much interference from Mom or Dad.

Some of us reach this point more gracefully than others. I had a casual friend in one of the apartment complexes where my son and I lived during his early teen years. This friend had a son two years older than mine. Throughout the son's early years, mother and son spent lots of time with each other. Both enjoyed sports and always attended games together. On the surface, they had a wonderfully close relationship. However, the teen had no privacy whatsoever. Even in his room, there was no "down time" between him and his mother.

One day, out of the blue, the teen told his mother to back off. He wanted some time to himself. Mom was

119

outraged. How could her teen treat her like that? After all, they were buddies, weren't they? No. In reality, they weren't buddies. They were adult and teen. The teen sensed this and wanted privacy from his mother.

At first, the mother panicked. What could he be doing in his room all by himself? There was no television, no electronic games, no radio. It was just the teen in a quiet room. What *could* he be doing?

He did nothing. He lay on the bed and thought. He sat on the floor and played with his toy soldiers. He composed songs. He wrote poetry. He did a number of things that his mother would have never given him credit for. He simply removed himself from her adult world and created one of his own.

Parents may not think that their teens are capable of functioning without them. They may prefer to think that every minute of every day must be planned lest their teenagers cease to exist. Regardless of what we may *want* to think, however, privacy is important to teenagers. It can be an opportunity to "chill out" in peace; a chance to think, experience emotional renewal, or find mental stimulation; a gradual sampling of independence. Teenagers need to be able to withdraw voluntarily from a complicated world and begin the process of making sense of it. "Leave me alone!" is a teen's way of saying, "Let me try to function on my own."

This is a legitimate request, and parents need to respect it. That doesn't mean teens have tickets to ride anywhere they wish. Teenagers who are still learning about privacy need to learn what we can tell them about enjoying privacy responsibly. But if we do not respect our teen's demand for privacy, then privacy is likely to become exactly what we are afraid it will: an opportunity to hide from problems that neither teen nor parent has been able to handle; a tool for concealing what was said or done; a habitual response to conflict; a tool for punishing; or a means of pushing parents away.

The Room Syndrome

Many teenagers spend their private moments in physical isolation. Teens barricade themselves in specific rooms where their privacy can be enforced by turning the key, placing a chair under the doorknob, or piling books or clothing against the door. Parents and others cannot come in without the teen's permission. Some rooms are better than others. Among the better rooms are:

Bathrooms Teenage boys close the door and sit on the pot, reflecting on life's inner meanings or doing their homework until it's time for them to graduate.

Teenage girls fuss with their make-up, hair, and clothing until the new fall fashions are introduced for next year.

The door is closed, and everyone in the home is affected—parents, siblings, relatives, even house guests. Etiquette is held hostage. Adults lose their tempers; other family members become distraught, frustrated, and maniacal. Relatives point fingers, while guests let you know that *their* teen would never do such a thing.

Parents must be very careful not to let their teens use bathrooms (or any other common room, for that matter) as control centers. Once locked in, teens will use the bathroom as a private refuge while everyone else suffers. Other places work better.

Bedrooms Yes, it is your house. But it is not your bedroom. Like it or not, your teen's bedroom is off-limits to your meddling, snooping, and trespassing (as teens put it).

Don't even think about changing the decorations. Posters, pictures, and other assorted trappings are for your teens and their friends.

My teen's grandmother once forgot how private a bedroom must be. She only needed a single reminder. A life-size poster of Ms. Pin-Up-of-the-Month was prominently displayed on the back of the door. She was enraged that her grandson indulged in such filth. I could only advise her to get her grandson's permission before entering his bedroom next time (and not to look).

Other Rooms Teens will use any room for privacy. It doesn't matter where the room is as long as it provides two thing: seclusion and solitude. Any old port in the storm, so to speak. The kitchen, the living room, the attic, even your bedroom (especially when they want privacy on the telephone) will suffice. Teens are not that particular.

Privacy Outside

When teens can't find privacy inside the house, they may seek it outside. They can even find privacy in a crowd.

Restaurants Teens collect in them until the place closes down around them. Restaurants are social lodges where teens can discuss their inner lives and mysteries without being disturbed or having their privacy violated by adults, siblings, or parents.

Teens seek collective privacy in the restaurant. They go in with the gang or meet the gang there and talk freely without interruption from the adult world. This allows them a "put-em-on-hold" privacy which helps teenagers come to terms with specific problems or concerns. This is also a "no-responsibility" privacy. Within this teenage fortress, parents and adults can not enforce the rules and regulations of the household or the community.

This is normal and usually healthy. It can go too far, however. I knew one teen who went to a local Bar-and-Grill every day after school for a single cup of coffee. He nursed this cup of coffee until the place shut down at ten PM. He claimed that his most productive hours were spent watching people without having people disturb him. The privacy of the greasy spoon was a retreat from family, friends, and schoolwork.

By itself, this would not be remarkable. But in this particular case it was privacy taken to an extreme. This teen didn't want the responsibility of dealing with his life, so mentally he hid out in order to avoid it. This privacy became destructive because it didn't solve anything in the long run. It only prolonged the agony that came from refusing to deal with his reality or that of his parents.

Walks When life becomes overwhelming, teens often take privacy walks. These walks may be at night without the benefit of a flashlight or street lights. With dark clothes on, too. Privacy is insured because no parent wants to join them (at three in the morning) and few can even see them once they've stepped outside.

When teens come home after several hours, don't ask, "Where have you been?" They won't tell you, because they really haven't been anywhere and, anyway, they don't want to.

"Everything okay?" you inquire.

"Sure, why do you ask?" your teen replies.

"Oh, just out of habit," you respond.

End of discussion.

This is an example of *evasive* privacy, something teens are quite adept at. You will seldom receive a straight answer when your teen doesn't want to give you one. It's like going through the funhouse at a carnival. Wherever you turn, you end up back where you started. Or worse. You may never really find out why your teen took the walk in the first place.

Private Property

Bookbags And School Papers Privacy also applies to intellectual property, including bookbags, papers, and whatever is inside the pages of text and library books. You may
consider this material to be lost and found, but your teen
is likely to consider it classified and/or privileged information.

My teen first demanded that I get permission to go
into his bookbag when he was eleven.

"What are you doing?" he asked as I began to place my
hand into the bag one morning.

"I'm looking for unsubmitted homework, missing permission forms, and overdue library books."

"Well, get out. Your hand doesn't belong in there." I
stared at him.

"What did you say?"

"You heard me. You have no right to go through my bag
unless I give you permission. You wouldn't want me to go
through your purse without your permission, would you?"

He had me. No, I wouldn't want him to go through my
things. They were my personal property. My teen felt the
same way. His bag was his personal property.

A little shaken, I left the room. Later, my teen came
over and handed me the bag.

"Next time, just ask. Now, do you want to go through
my bag?"

"Sure, why not," I answered, and put my hand in.

I did find some embarrassing things: a permission
form for a field trip that should have been signed two
weeks ago; a homework page that should have been
turned in last week; a lunch from three weeks ago. Except
for those things, there was nothing interesting to find. My
fingers did come out black-blue, however, from his dam-
aged fountain pen.

Some teens have told me that their parents almost never check their bags while other teens say that their parents give "spot" or "surprise" inspections just to keep them on their toes. Don't look unless you are willing to find something you don't want to find or risk creating an uncomfortable confrontation.

For example, one mother found a "Love Appointment Book" while looking through her teenage daughter's bookbag. Inside the book were love letters from friends. Marked on each love letter was an appointment date, and each appointment date was entered in the book next to the boy's name.

The girl was furious. How could her mother be so nosey? The mother was livid. How could her daughter do this? Her daughter was much too young. Maybe. But the mother had no business looking through her daughter's stuff without asking her daughter first.

Telephones The phone rings. Your teen shouts, "I'll get it," and dashes to pick it up. Once on the phone, he or she turns around and asks, "Well?"

This is a clue from your teen. Phone privacy is nothing to be trifled with. Your teen expects you to leave the room...as if you didn't have anything better to do than listen in on the phone conversation. Your teen's privacy is threatened. The enemy is you.

To be honest, some parents do eavesdrop on their kid's conversations. Their excuses may range from "It's for your own good" to "It's not that I don't trust you, but..." Whatever your reasons for eavesdropping may be, remember that in future years your teen will emulate your behavior, perhaps even when you are on the phone. Do you want *your* calls monitored? No one does.

Phone calls are personal communications between your teen and a friend, another adult, or a possible employer. There's no need for parents to hang around in hallways or door entries, listen in on a second phone, or quiz another sibling. Don't force your teen to lie about or cover up a phone conversation. Don't sell your kids short. Your teen will share the information later with you if he feels it concerns you or if she really wants you to be involved.

Mail Eventually, your teen will begin to receive party invitations, school report cards, and all sorts of mail from friends, adults, advertisers, and promoters.

Teens demand and deserve the same privacy with their mail as with the phone. No one likes the privacy of their mail to be violated by anyone, concerned parents or otherwise.

A friend of mine was taught this lesson dramatically by a very frustrated daughter. The two happened to share the same first name. At first, this was no problem. But when the daughter became a teenager and began receiving letters from boyfriends, the situation changed.

The mother swore that she couldn't tell when mail was meant for her daughter, so she opened all the mail. After reading a few lines and realizing it wasn't her mail, she insisted she put the letters back and closed the envelope. These were innocent mistakes, she insisted.

The daughter suspected otherwise. Her mother was a busybody. The daughter's privacy was being violated. She asked her mom how she would like her mail opened intentionally every time.

"No way, kiddo," the mother indignantly said, "No way."

But she continued opening her daughter's letters. Out of desperation, the teen told her friends to address her letters to Sherry, her personal nickname. Still, the mother kept on opening her daughter's mail. No longer able to call it an innocent error, Mom now claimed that Sherry was too young to insist on privacy. She asserted the right, as a mother, to protect her daughter from life.

In desperation, Sherry held a war meeting with her friends. They wrote letters for her mother to open. Sherry's mom was looking for smut; she read smut. Sherry's mom was looking for illicit encounters; she was given dates, times, and locations. Sherry's mom was convinced that Sherry was on the pill; a package of birth control pills came with instructions and an authorized prescription from some clinic doctor.

It took some time, but Sherry's mom got the point. She finally stopped reading Sherry's mail.

Respecting Privacy

Privacy means a great deal to everyone, teenager and adult alike. It is a fundamental part of individuality and autonomy. The line separating respect for privacy from respect for the individual is pretty much imaginary.

Teens need and deserve privacy in their personal belongings, whether they are stored in school lockers, bedroom drawers, closets, or any other personal area. And they need to feel secure in their conversations and correspondence. Teens need to know that parents respect their privacy. Without privacy, communication suffers. Meddling parents often find that their kids are increasingly reluctant to share even the ordinary events of their lives. Why? Because to many teenagers, failure to respect privacy is the same thing as failure to respect the teen. Resentful teens understandably keep secrets from parents and others who they feel don't respect them.

Respecting privacy teaches your teen about the trust that is such an important component of adult behavior and a necessary part of a good parent-teen relationship. Trust your teen's judgment when they make or receive phone calls, get mail, or keep papers in their private areas. If there's a problem, your teens will come to you, unless you have driven them to secrecy by distrusting them and disrespecting their privacy.

Respecting your teenager's privacy does not mean "anything goes." Teens may know early what privacy is, but they need to learn what privacy is not. Privacy is not a one-way street. It is not something that is given or taken away as convenience dictates. It does not mean one thing for teens and another thing for everyone else. Privacy is not a license to do anything, an escape-hatch for teens to remove themselves from responsibility, a security blanket to protect them from the challenges of growing up, or a device to hide their irresponsible behavior from you.

You and your teen need to have a common understanding of what privacy is and what it implies. This understanding should be based on your existing relationship, but make sure it contains some or all of the following principles:

☞ Certain behaviors, areas, and possessions are "off limits" to both you and your teenager.

☞ Knocking and asking permission is the way to enter an off-limits area. Marching in unannounced is not.

☞ Eavesdropping or listening to someone else's private conversation is not appropriate behavior.

☞ Snooping through another's closets, drawers, lockers, or personal belongings or reading someone else's private material without permission is not acceptable.

☞ Respect for privacy must be reciprocal. Both you and your teen need to offer respect if you expect to receive respect. Neither of you should be pointing grubby fingers at villains. You may discover that you are pointing at the mirror.

☞ Privacy is not always a given. In some relationships, privacy must first be earned between parent and teen. Many teens demand privacy, but certain circumstances may prevent it from happening. Find a way to ensure that your teen has some kind of privacy, some kind of cubby hole he or she can call inviolate.

☞ Privacy is both a right and a responsibility. Make sure you all understand that and act accordingly.

Invading Privacy

For teenagers and parents alike, issues of privacy can challenge some of the foundations on which their relationship is built. Privacy should not be violated for trivial reasons. *It's for their own good.... We're just being on the safe side.... The kids won't mind.... We're doing them a favor by protecting them from themselves*—none of these by themselves justifies violating someone else's right to privacy, even if the violation is no more innocuous than rummaging through your teen's drawers while putting the laundry away. This victimizes your teenager just as you would be victimized if, perhaps by following your example, your teen helped himself or herself to the loose change on your dresser.

But every so often, privacy can turn into something that parents don't anticipate. Sometimes, privacy causes trouble. What happens when teen or parent discovers that the right to privacy cannot be respected? When teens feel they have to protect what they feel is nobody's business? When parents discover that they have to intrude on an area their teen considers sacred? Perhaps a teen has learned to lie in order to prevent parents from finding something out. Perhaps a teen has been living a double life, Billy Jekyll in the daytime and Brutus Hyde at night. What do you do when you find out? (And you *will* find out—there are too many outside sources of truth, including siblings, teachers, other parents, even friends of your teen.)

How should you respond, for example, when you discover that your thirteen-year-old daughter is secretly dating and sleeping with a twenty-one year old "man" with or without taking precautions? How do you react when you find out that your teenage son is part of a car-stripping ring or your teenage daughter is working for an "escort service" in the neighboring town?

At times like these, a teen must not be allowed to hide behind the right to privacy. After all that has been said about the importance of respecting a teen's privacy, how do you justify invading that privacy?

At times, justification may not be necessary. If your daughter is involved in a dangerous or life-threatening situation, you need to step in immediately. Her privacy is not nearly as important as her health or safety. Or your son may actually invite your intervention without asking for it. He may, for example, stage a "simulation" by mentioning offhandedly that he has this friend who is doing this or struggling with that. Then, he'll await your instructions breathlessly, relieved that he never had to admit to you that it was he who needed the help.

At other times, however, the justification might not be so clear. What do you do, for example, when you find contraband in your teenager's room? I discussed this with parents, substance-abuse counselors, and teens who had been caught hiding such things as alcohol, cigarettes, drugs, and birth-control paraphernalia among their personal belongings. The consensus was overwhelming:

- ☞ Remember your real reason for going through your teen's personal belongings. Is it because you suspect something? Is your child behaving erratically? Were you tipped off that something wasn't right?
- ☞ Don't lie to yourself or to your teen. Be honest and open, even though it may be painful. As parents, you've got to

know what the problem is, even if you don't want to. Face it together.

☞ Don't blow your cool. Remain calm. Make sure something really is wrong before you act. Don't simply confront your teen and push the stuff under his or her nose. Nothing will be solved that way. The teenager will only deny the crime. "How did that get here? You know me. I don't do drugs. I'm just keeping it safe for Joe Blow. He's my best friend. You don't want me to rat on my best friend, do you?"

☞ Ask if your teen has anything that he or she would like to talk to you about. Ask how school is going, what is happening with him or her, or anything else that you as the parent should know. Respond to the cues your teen gives you.

☞ Give your child time to respond. Maybe he or she will tell you that the gang is trying smoking together, that someone brought in a joint and that they all passed it around just to see what would happen, that someone bought a bottle of liquor and they experimented with it. Don't judge immediately.

☞ Listen to what your teen tells you in reply. It is important to understand *why* in addition to *what*. Is this a one-time event or is it becoming a habit?

☞ If your teen doesn't tell you directly, don't try to force a confession. Announce that you found something while you were putting clothes away, then name what you found exactly. Don't apologize; you are the parent and your teen is the teenager.

☞ If there's a problem, work it out together.

☞ Make sure that your teenager understands any legal ramifications, even if it is a first offense. What may have happened when you were growing up no longer applies: taking things from retail stores is now considered shoplifting and punished with fines and imprisonment; getting freebies without paying for them is considered stealing, whether it's a meal or a comic book. Taking drugs is not just another harmless recreational activity. Society continues to change its attitudes about such things. Make sure your teenager realizes that joyriding, hot-rodding, and speed racing are stupid acts to pull. Someone always gets hurt. Just hand them the local paper.

Police Shoot Fleeing Teenager

Three Teenagers Killed Trying To Outrace Train, Drinking Blamed

Teenager On Drugs Crashes Into Van, Mother And Child Killed

The stories go on. If only more headlines would read:

Teenager Alive Because Parents Invaded Privacy

It's difficult for parents to decide to go through their teen's property. Is it the right thing to do? It's not easy to count on your relationship with your teenager to help the teen get over the resentment of having his or her belongings ransacked. It's not any easier to ask your teenager outright whether he or she has been driving on the right or the wrong side of the street. But sometimes, these things have to be done.

It's impossible to demand responsibility from a teenager when the teen is not ready for it or unable to shake off outside forces that the teen can't control. Parents must learn how far their teenagers can be trusted with the *responsibility* of privacy. Privacy can be abused, but it can also be respected. So much depends on how the parent handled it in the past and the foundation their teenagers have received during their preteen years.

As a parent, you are the adult. Your teenager is your charge at least until he or she is old enough to leave home. No one likes to be spied upon or to have their belongings searched, but if something is truly for the good of the teenager or the family, then it must be done. No matter how painful it may be for a teenager, you have to exercise your own responsibilities. You are a parent first, not a friend. No one else can draw the lines as clearly as you can.

Years from now, your teenager will thank you.

CHAPTER 11

The Teenage Playroom

Small kids play in playrooms, safe places built by parents where children can play without concern for the consequences of their playing. Within the bounded area of the playroom, the children decide what is true and false, right and wrong, good and bad. For many small children, playrooms are early laboratories of real life.

Teens play in metaphorical playrooms, with many of the same results. Teen playrooms are also built by parents. They form the realm of freedom which the parents allow, the behaviors that teenagers can practice and the discretion which they can exercise. In their playrooms, teenagers learn to stand on their own and find their own terms for relating to the world. Playrooms are parts of the process in which teens become adults.

The "walls" of the playroom are the rules for living, the boundaries that separate acceptable and unacceptable behavior and keep teens from diving head-first into the deep end of the wading pool. Parents set the rules, but teens must accept them. Teenagers and parents tacitly cooperate in defining the boundaries that form appropriate walls. For teens, playrooms are safe zones where they can learn how to function in society, secure in knowing that their parents are standing there to protect them from making really bad decisions. For parents, the playroom is an island of restraint where they can maintain some supervision over their teens and keep them from doing dumb things.

As teens frolic in their playrooms, the passage through the teenage years is marked by those events, both small and large, that are the milestones of their journey from the world of the child to the world of the adult. These moments and events are the "doorways" to the playroom. At each portal, a teen can choose to move through the doorway, step back into the safety of the playroom, or stay put and watch. As each doorway is negotiated, the walls of the playroom expand. Each doorway is a moment of growth, and with growth, the playroom gets larger.

When a teen encounters a doorway, the teen exercises a choice. What a teen does at each doorway reflects the teen's maturity on the one hand and chutzpah on the other. Whether a teen boldly strides forward, slinks back to safety, or stands motionless in the middle of the doorway like a cat confronting another feline on the other side of the screen depends on how ready and willing the teen is to move forward.

Parents need to encourage teens to make choices at these doorways, even contradictory choices. After all, the very act of choosing is part of learning how to take on responsibility. Making a choice willingly is an important sign that a teen is making progress.

The Teenager's Challenge

Most teens appreciate the structure and framework of the playroom. They may seem restless or uncomfortable, but most are secretly delighted that they have playrooms to grow in and are not simply thrown into the real world. My son once confided in me that he was glad he didn't have to act responsibly, even though he was aware that there was a big difference between our individual ideas about what responsible behavior actually was. The adult world was challenging, he told me, but also very frightening. There were too many decisions to make, too much discipline involved. What if his choices turned out wrong? He was not ready to make the jump from one side to the other. He was relieved that Mom still acted as the heavy and carried part of his responsibility for him. He liked the fact that he could peek through his doorways and take in the fascinating and terrifying adult world on the other side without actually having to step into it.

Many teens do not share my son's perspective. They may not acknowledge that they are playing in playrooms or even recognize that playrooms exist. Teens are often oblivious to a fact that is apparent to just about everyone else: playroom play is a form of safe experimentation. Many teens consider their playroom behavior as an assertion of their inherent right to exercise personal authority and control. Unfortunately, these inherent rights do not exist in a teenager's vacuum. Teens need playrooms so they can learn that what they do affects others. Playrooms are one of the few safe ways to learn this by doing.

Teens are often confused about what being an adult really means. Many have to learn that it is not just a free ride. Learning how to be an adult means learning how to make good judgments and intelligent choices. Having a playroom to play in gives teens experiences that informed judgments and choices can be based on. It is unrealistic to expect that your teen will simply know that something can have bad consequences. Teens need to learn to think things through, to realize that things can go wrong even with the best of plans and intentions. Playrooms give them practice.

Parents shouldn't meddle in their teen's lives—as if their teens would let them even if they tried. But it is important that parents pay attention to the kinds of playroom judgments and choices their kids are making. Consider what happened to one local teen. She and two teenage boys were drawn together by a shared love of drama, particularly famous death scenes from stage and film. Theatrical suicides, gun shots, stabbings, drug overdoses, all provided fertile ground for their overactive and recklessly passionate imaginations.

One day, the girl decided to reenact the scene of her life—almost literally. She would take Ophelia's suicide in Hamlet one step further. First, she would go mad from a pill "overdose." Then, instead of throwing herself into the stream and drowning, she would "hang" herself with a leather belt suspended from a pipe in the school basement. Her two friends shared her excitement. They printed and distributed fliers around the school so that the entire student body would be invited to view this crowning event of her theatrical career.

Fortunately for her, one of her friends told a trusted adult what was going to happen. The adult urged them not to go ahead with a stunt that was clearly beyond their capability. Of course, they didn't listen; after all, it was all going to happen entirely as planned. The play went on. The girl almost strangled. Their adult friend saved the day. All three friends were sorry. It never occurred to them that something might go wrong. If someone hadn't been there to watch over their playroom, something would have. The kids were fortunate that an adult showed interest in what they were doing. It is a shame that the interested adult was not one of their parents.

Adulthood Isn't Built in a Day

It is not unusual for teens to push on the boundaries of their playrooms. For some, the thrill of the challenge is hard to resist; for others, the impatience is difficult to ignore. Almost all teens step over the bounds, embarrass themselves, and, we hope, crawl sheepishly back into the safety of the playroom.

Most teens challenge boundaries, often openly. Defiance for the sake of defiance is a widely shared teenage habit. For many, the reasons for playroom restraint are not always apparent. Obedience becomes a form of shackle and disobedience becomes an assertion that *I don't need no playroom.* To many teens, the outlaw is a role model, especially when other teens are around. "So I hitched. Big deal. You did it!" (So did every soldier, sailor, hippie, and bum between here and Moosebreath County.) The fact that times have changed since you hitched doesn't sink in, and probably wouldn't make much difference if it did.

When (not if) your teen does this, stay calm. The last thing he or she needs is a panic-filled tirade from an incensed and irrational parent. Your teen knows that he or she made a mistake, even if it really was an accident. Simply lording it over your teen won't accomplish anything. Instead, sit down with your teen and discuss what happened. Make sure that you reaffirm the boundaries of the playroom without lecturing, humiliating, haranguing, or saying, "I told you so."

Expect your teen to offer some resistance, some justification, some excuse. When several local teenagers were caught bashing curbside mailboxes with baseball bats, for example, their response was, "There was nothing else to do." Other predictable excuses include: "Everyone else is doing it; It's not hurting anyone; It's just all clean, innocent fun; I'm just going through a phase;" and "It's not like I did it on purpose, or anything."

Teens need to know that excuses like these don't make irresponsible behavior acceptable. Playrooms allow teens to practice adult behavior before they have to take full responsibility for their actions. You are there to help them, protect them, shield them, and make it possible for them to make mistakes they can learn from. You are not there to give carte blanche to their self-indulgences. After all, in some places parents are actually held responsible for the misdeeds of their kids. And you are not going to be there forever. At some point, teens must learn to govern themselves.

For a few teens, playrooms seem like unacceptable confinements. These are the teens who dynamite play-room walls instead of walking through doors. Perhaps they are stealing money from your wallet or purse for drugs or alcohol; perhaps they are lying about their behavior; perhaps they are cutting school without permission or slipping out of the house in the middle of the night; perhaps they are charging unapproved purchases on your credit cards; perhaps they are having automobile accidents or speeding tickets. Whatever the symptoms, these hardened playroom criminals need firmer restraint and perhaps even outside help. Kids who don't learn responsible behavior while they have a playroom to play in may never learn to act responsibly.

Learning To Be Adults

In the normal course of a teenage life, playrooms gradually expand and walls slowly break down. By the end of their teenage years, most kids have stepped through all the doorways and learned to stand in the open air. But not all teens make this journey according to the same schedule.

Teens become adults at their own speeds. The only accurate generalization about playrooms may be that the older the teenager becomes, the more difficult it is for the teen to accept the balance between freedom and restraint that playrooms offer. The earlier you introduce your teen to playrooms, the sooner your teen will learn to handle expanded walls and the better able your teen will be to deal with the adult world.

There are no clear-cut stages of evolution or hard-and-fast rules for progressing through the playroom years. Different teens need different playrooms. Appropriate playrooms are built around the emotional and mental maturity of each individual teen. Some teens blossom immediately, making it easy for parents to enlarge the playroom boundaries; others are tentative, reticent, or irresponsible. Some welcome the challenge; others look back for guidance.

Your teen will let you know—probably often—that the playroom feels too small. You, the parent, need to know your teenager well enough to determine exactly how much to expand the realm of sheltered freedom. Like it or not, you need to be there in the playroom with your teen if only to know how much additional discretion your teen is ready to take on.

Sometimes a playroom doorway just materializes, forcing you and your teen to adjust, ready or not. These are often unsettling or uncomfortable experiences, but ones from which your teen can learn valuable lessons.

"Mom," my son told me one evening, "we have a problem."

"What do you mean *we*? What is the problem?"

"Sam and his date are here. He drove his date's car over. It's the one her parents rented. He doesn't have his license with him. And his date is too drunk to drive. Her parents aren't home, and if they were, they'd kill her because they don't know she took the rented car."

"What is she doing with a rented car anyway? She's only eighteen, and no one under twenty-one is supposed to be driving a rented car. Besides, Sam doesn't even have a regular license—only a learner's permit. I'd say Sam and his date have the problem."

Sam and his date had abused the situation. They got into trouble and had to turn to an adult—me, via my son—to get them out of the swamp they had marched into with their eyes open. The lure of an adult's freedom can be deceptive and intoxicating, especially to teens who are not there yet.

Still, this was a doorway for Sam, his date, and my son. Why? Because they learned a valuable lesson about becoming an adult as a result of their problem. Even though they did not solve the problem themselves (*Thank Goodness!*), they still came through the episode with a little more knowledge about adult choices and decisions.

At other times, doorways are passed without being noticed. You wake up one morning and discover that your teen is older. "Midterms are coming up, and there's no way I'm going to take them all in one or two days. So I rearranged my schedule to take one test a day. This leaves me time to study and mess around. What do you think of that?"

My son once came home from a night out, swaggering as if he had just taken the video-game championship away from the guy who had held it for years. "I went out with the guys. They drank and made fools of themselves, just like they always do. I drove them all home and explained to their parents why they were drunk and I wasn't. You should've been there!"

Playrooms And Relationships

Playrooms also give teens a chance to learn how to develop good relationships with others. In the playroom, teens experience the full spectrum of social relationships. These are necessary if sometimes painful experiences. Teens often make assumptions about others that adults have learned not to make (or fail to make assumptions that adults know should be made). The playroom helps teens learn how to judge others and how to build relationships on more than superficial bases.

When my teen was seventeen, he came home with three antique knives—I never did find out who in their right mind would sell knives like these to minors—and a couple of casual friends. He was at that point in the life of a male teenager when weapons like knives hold a powerful, macho appeal. These weapons, of course, are never dangerous. They are decorative extensions of a teen's identity and a privilege to which teens are entitled.

He assured me that these knives were only for "show and tell." I believed him; after all, he was seventeen and he knew the rules. I had nothing to fear, he promised. Of course, he couldn't speak for the friends he brought over. These kids casually ran their fingers over the blades to see how sharp the knives were and tested their throwing balance to hear the sound a sixteen-inch blade made when it was thrown against a wall or a wooden chest of drawers. Their assurance of "Just kidding!" didn't undo the damage, but it did let my teen see that friendship is more than just a common interest in things like weapons. It was *his* wall and *his* chest of drawers.

Teens start and end relationships on things like that. They have to make mistakes. That's how they grow, usually at their expense and sometimes at yours. Playrooms help them learn how to handle relationships while you are still there to steer them in the right directions.

As your teen grows, don't be surprised to find old friends on the way out and new ones taking their places. Teens play in their own playrooms. Sometimes the play-rooms become so different that once inseparable pals end up following totally different paths. Sometimes, kids who were opposites in every respect become best buddies. It is not unusual for a teen's world to be disrupted dramatically as he or she marches through playroom doorways. This disruption, in turn, becomes yet another doorway for the teen to pass through.

"At first, we were a team," one teen told me. "There wasn't anything we couldn't do together, see together, and have fun with. But things changed. I didn't expect their brother to crash, but he did. He flunked the first semester in college. Then he came home. And he stayed home, messing around and losing every job he got. His brothers sort of picked up this *give-up* message from him. One went to a rinky-dink college and the other really did give up. Why not? His older brother did it, so why not him? All he does now is sit around drinking, smoking, and hanging out. He's like a bad sore—you keep picking at it so it never heals. Who needs that? Not me! I'm for bigger things in life. I don't need someone else to drag me down. So I split."

In their playrooms, teens learn to take responsibility for the contributions they make to their relationships. It is easy for everyone, not just teenagers, to treat relationships as one-way streets and answers to the question *What's in it for me?* During their teenage year, kids have the opportunity to build lasting relationships on firm foundations. They may never have as promising an opportunity again.

Playrooms And Parents

Parents are in the playroom, too. Your relationship with your teen will change as the playroom expands. Your teen is growing. That little bundle of joy you used to rock to sleep is getting closer to adulthood, the end of the teenage journey and the beginning of the autonomous life. Your child, one day soon, is not going to be a child any longer.

Not all parents are prepared for this metamorphosis. For many, a child is always a child. These parents often have difficulty accepting that the things that go on in the playroom are anything more than pages in the scrap book. For teens, on the other hand, the teenage years are a series of high points that mark their increasing differentiation from their parents and their progress toward a life of their own.

Remember that autonomy and independence are goals that almost all teenagers pursue. "I wanted to live the first year away from home," said one college-bound teenager, "preferably in the dorms. The only way to do this was to get a job. My parents blew a gasket. I got a job, one I didn't like. My parents were almost happy. 'Bad choice,' they said. 'Too young,' they said. 'Come home where you belong.' But I'm stubborn, you know? So I kept visiting the job board at Student Services, and I found a job that I really like. The only part that I don't enjoy is working on weekends and holidays and being expected to punch in on a time clock. But, I need the bucks. And, like they say, it looks good on my résumé."

Your teen is maturing, changing, growing, becoming more sophisticated. Your relationship with your teen has to change. Don't cling to the past—it is gone. Don't try to shape the future—you couldn't do that even if your teenager let you try. You and your teen have an evolving relationship; let that relationship take its own form. If your mutual relationship is strong, the passage through the playroom can be a positive event for both of you.

You and your teen can use the playroom to shape the course of your relationship. When Gregory graduated from high school, for example, he and his parents reached a crossroads. He was no longer a student, but he still lived at home. He had reached a new stage in his growth—the proto-adult stage. Gregory was bringing home a pretty decent check every week from his summer job, and his parents thought it was time for him to take on some adult responsibility.

"Here's the deal," they said. Gregory could continue living at home, but he would have to help out with room and board. Gregory was aghast. It wasn't fair, he protested. Why should graduating from high school make such a difference? He was still a kid. He couldn't even vote, and he had only recently gotten his license. All he wanted to do was save his money for college, and this didn't help. What were they trying to do, ruin his shot at college success? Nothing had happened to justify this kind of change! His friends agreed. How could his parents be such rats? They must be out to get him.

One of Gregory's girl friends came up with a teenager's answer: move out of his home and move into her house. *Her* parents were cool. They wouldn't make him spend all his money on little things like room and board. Her parents agreed; they had plenty of room and didn't mind an extra body. So Gregory got ready to move in.

Gregory didn't understand that he would be expected to work for his room and board. When the girl's parents explained the arrangement, his own parents didn't seem like such ogres after all. Gregory called home a few hours later and asked if they could discuss this room-and-board thing again. Gregory began to see that adulthood wasn't like being a kid, and he realized reluctantly that it was going to be a little more complicated than he had thought.

Teens are going to push at walls and walk through doorways with or without their parents' approval. No one loses as long as no one clings to the notion that doorways are to be closed and locked forever or the notion that they are to be rushed through indiscriminately. Your teen needs both the freedom and the security that a playroom can offer.

Eventually, the playroom has to disappear, usually by mutual consent. Someday, your son or daughter is going to come to you and say, "You don't understand. It's worth ten dollars to me. You just don't find copies of Number 6 *The X-Men* in this condition." At some point, you have to accept this logic and get out of the way.

What you can do before that happens is encourage your teen and help him or her prepare for what comes next. Walking through the doorways to the world outside can be a frightening yet exhilarating challenge. Your teen needs your support to develop the self-confidence to undertake the passage. Your teen also needs to know that if things don't go as he or she planned, you are there in case he or she needs you. For a while, give your teen the best of both worlds, opportunity with security.

The successful mastery of a playroom is measured by accomplishments, but the meaning of these accomplishments is not always evident. Your teen is only now learning how to judge the real significance of things. He or she needs you now as much as ever. Talk with your teen about what is happening. Review events and discuss what it was like before and what your teen's life is likely to be in the future. Your teen may need you to acknowledge the playroom triumphs. Do it.

Don't push your teen through the doorways. Allow your teen to go through the doors according to his or her own schedule. Impatience won't help; your teen will take the step when it feels right. And don't compare your teen's progress to that of another teen. Doorways are maturing moments, and different teens mature at different paces. Some can do at fifteen what others cannot do at eighteen. Trust that the doorways are there and that your teen will go through them.

As your teen matures and the playroom grows, you will notice the difference. Each milestone your teen passes will be your milestone, too. You will gain as your teen pushes the walls wider. Remember that you are sharing this playroom with your teen. By paying attention to what your teen is doing, you stay more in touch with your kid's day-to-day life. He or she may not always appreciate sharing the playroom with you; your teen may well feel as if you are always enforcing arbitrary rules and regulations. But your teen needs the assurance that you are there in case you are needed. Later on, when your teen discovers that the world is full of rules and regulations that someone is always enforcing, he or she will understand that you really weren't always in their face.

For parents, playrooms bring their own joys. One of the greatest is the pride that comes from watching a teen—your teen—enter the playroom as a child and come out as an adult.

CHAPTER 12

Mistakes

Teenagers make mistakes. They learn by doing.

Mistakes cause discomfort. They put teens in compromising positions they would rather not be in, admit, or face. Mistakes force teens to choose: *Should I tell the truth, stall, or pretend it didn't happen at all?* Teenagers make mistakes for several different reasons: lack of judgment, inadequate knowledge, and inattention to the facts or problem right in front of them are three of the most common. Parents often compound the discomfort by delivering their advice in lecture form. This only focuses the attention on the teens' mistakes. Parents jump to conclusions and assume what happened even before the teen can explain it. Parents also almost always use an *it's different* argument to shield themselves and pull. Parents are very much like their teenage offspring—they'll never admit (at least not openly) that they make mistakes, too.

Between Parent And Teen

Mistakes are a "relationship thing" as one teen put it, or "combat fatigue" in the words of another. The problem often belongs to the parents, many of whom have trouble accepting their teens' failures. Parents may feel attacked. They may become annoyed when their teens make the same mistake again and again. All too often they waste their breath on minor mistakes. Then, when teens take more serious missteps, they have already been antagonized by the previous criticisms. When parents have gone to the well too often, they dilute the constructive impact their criticism can have. It becomes difficult for parents to communicate their legitimate worry, concern, or advice in any form once their teens have become numbed to their suggestions. They have heard all this before, so why listen now?

Poor Judgment

No one likes to think of themselves as witless or stupid, yet many teens get trapped in that kind of thinking simply because they just don't take the time to think things through. George, for example, liked to volunteer himself for missions. Whenever any of his friends needed help, he was there. But he didn't always think before he acted, and the results often went awry.

One evening George received a phone call from a friend. She was stuck at school and needed a ride home. Even though George was at work when he received the call, he decided to give his friend the ride. He didn't bother to call home to notify his parents about his change of plans.

He also didn't bother to consider whether it was a good idea. It was snowing. It was icy. George's car was not winterized. In fact, it didn't have a heater, a defroster, snow tires, good brakes, or working headlights. Still, George felt the call of responsibility.

By the time he picked up his friend, the storm had made the streets dangerous. The snow plows had been too busy with the interstates and main roads to pay any more than minimal attention to the side streets. George didn't see the divider in the middle of the road until he hit it. The car died right there. An unsympathetic policeman gave George thirty minutes to remove the car from the street if he didn't want it to be towed.

George finally called his parents who picked the two teens up in time to get a stern tongue-lashing from the police. *What kind of parent would let an inexperienced sixteen-year-old teen driver loose on snowy streets?* The girl friend got home around midnight. George and his parents spent the rest of the night arguing about what George did and what he should have done.

Lack Of Knowledge

Teens claim to know everything. Even parents (who do know everything) have a rough time convincing their teens that they are overlooking something.

Just before my teen and his friend were supposed to pick up their prom dates, I asked them, "Do both of you know the way there?"

"Yes. Stop nagging. We'll be fine."

"Okay. Take an extra quarter just in case."

He was convinced that he knew best, so I stopped lecturing. Two hours later, He called. I was not surprised.

"Hello, Mom? We took a wrong turn. We're at the airport."

"Wait a second. What time do you need to pick up your dates?"

"*Uh*...well...*uh*...we're about...*uh*...we're running... *uh*...late."

"How late?" I asked.

"Oh, about an hour's worth."

"Did you call them?"

"No. We'll get there."

Three hours later, the dates were calling to find out where their escorts were.

On another occasion, I received a phone call from my teen. He was trapped in the hospital parking lot, and was calling from the toll booth.

"It really is true. If you don't have the money to get out, they won't let you leave the parking lot!"

Inattention

Teens also make mistakes because they are not paying attention to what should be obvious. It is not always their fault; things that are obvious to someone who has "been there" may not be so obvious to someone who has not "done that." On the other hand, sometimes it is. Teens don't always want to pay attention. It is a lot of work and not immediately gratifying.

Friends and property are two places where errors of attention are likely to occur. When property and friends are involved at the same time, the probability of a mistake happening multiplies. For example, teenagers often loan their own and other people's property to other teens, not always with the best of outcomes. My teen was a sucker for teens who "absolutely needed" his books. "Trust me. I'll return this library book for you as soon as I am done."

Right.

"I know Jed turned in that library book."

"Are you sure?" I asked for the umpteenth time.

"Why doesn't the library believe me?"

Once, my teen shared his iron-clad logic about loaning things to his friends.

"I told him it was okay to borrow it," my teen said.

"You told whom what was okay?" I replied.

"A friend," stressed my teen.

"Do you know the kid's name?" I asked.

"No. I trust him," came the retort. "Look, I don't have to ask for it back. He'll know when it's time to return it."

"By the way, what did you loan him?"

"My English textbook."

"When does the book have to be returned?"

"I don't know."

"Can't you ask and find out?"

"It's not done that way."

My teen reassured me. "The book will be returned before the end of the school year."

Oh well. My teen paid for the book out of his allowance. Live and learn.

Part of learning to recognize the obvious is to learn how to anticipate the consequences of screwing up.

"I misplaced my permission slip. You haven't seen it, have you?"

"No, not recently. Why?"

"I need it for the field trip tomorrow."

"When did you get the permission slip."

"About two weeks ago. Why?"

Conflicts between school and job can be quite common.

"Did I tell you I have to work tonight?"

"That's nice. Don't you have a test tomorrow?"

"I'm ready."

"Good."

"I also have a paper. Six pager. You wouldn't want to stay up a little later tonight to do some typing, would you?"

"No, but you will. Have a nice evening!"

Mistake Quotas

When teens seem confused or bewildered, they often are. Mistakes and screw-ups, all too common under normal conditions, multiply when life looms larger. Be prepared, and be just a little more generous with your patience.

"I remembered that it got done. It's in here somewhere, all right? Give me a moment to collect my thoughts."

Often, a teen's reasoning may sound half-witted—even to teens themselves (though they won't admit it).

"Some guy called."

"Did you get his name, number, and message?"

"I thought you knew all that stuff. I'll get it when he calls back."

Teens may learn from previous experience, but not always right away. Like it or not, sometimes you can't help but get involved.

"I was tempted to sign your name at the bottom of the permission form, but I didn't."

"I'm glad to hear that."

"I decided that it was too risky."

"Delighted."

"However, I did tell them that you wouldn't mind."

"I wouldn't mind what?"

"Baking the cookies. Three hundred of 'em. You're such a pal."

Other Mistakes

Some mistakes don't just happen. A teen may anticipate the misstep but ignore the warning signs and proceed blindly forward. It's easier. Besides, the mistake is worth the risk and challenge.

It's one AM and you are in bed. The phone rings. The teenager on the other end wants to speak to your teen. Your daughter told her to call.

There's a teen standing outside your door. You think you know who he is, but you're not sure. Your son went out for the night, but he told this guy to come by tonight and he'd return something he'd borrowed.

Has your teen ever volunteered to do the laundry? You explain patiently how the whites, colors, and cold temperature clothing are washed separately. When you come home, you find that the clothes have all been washed in one temperature in one large load. "It saves on water."

Compound Mistakes

Not all mistakes made by teenagers are as frivolous or simple as these. Sometimes, teens get into situations where they can do serious damage. The combination of poor judgment, poor knowledge, and poor attention can be deadly.

"I came to a dead stop behind this car, and this other guy drives into my side of the car. Luckily, the cop agreed with me. There was no way I was at fault, not if I had tried."

"I didn't see the car. It must have moved just when it saw me back out. It wasn't there when I started."

"I really thought he would go around me. I never thought he would just keep coming at me."

"I thought I would go for a walk. I got off from work early and drove to the Reservation and parked the car. Somewhere, down the path, I felt something slide through my right pocket. At the time I wasn't thinking clearly, so I didn't do anything about it. When I got back to the car, I felt for my keys. They were gone! That must've been what slipped through my trouser pocket. Well, I was in the woods when this happened. I ran back to where I thought I lost them and looked all over the place, but I didn't have a flashlight. It was eleven o'clock by then. I was going crazy. Luckily, there was a pay phone there, so I called Carl to come and pick me up. When I stepped out of the phone booth, I felt something in my left trouser pocket. Guess what? My car keys were there. Was I relieved. That's why I'm late. Sorry. It won't happen again."

Only Sweat The Big Stuff

Teenagers are going to make thoughtless, silly, and terrible mistakes. It's part of being a teenager. Don't get too rattled by the little ones. In fact, encourage them. It is the only way your teen is going to learn.

When it isn't small stuff, there are things parents can do to help teenagers deal with their mistakes. Above all, encourage teens to tell the truth, no matter how painful it might be. Make them sit down and take a few deep breaths. Then encourage them to start at the beginning and, in their own words, explain what really happened. Whatever you hear, don't interrupt the explanations. Interruptions are confusing and insulting. Don't put teens on the defensive—you may never learn the truth if you do.

Focus on the important points and clarify them so that everyone agrees about the basic facts. Discuss what happened, why it happened, and how to avoid it in the future. Don't lecture, scold, point fingers, or say, "I told you so!" This can only alienate teenagers when what you really want is for teens to confide in you and ask for your advice.

Parents are fortunate when their teens make their worst mistakes while still living at home. They can be there to guide their kids through the difficulties. Your teens need to listen to you and to benefit from your experience. The next time they make similar mistakes, you want them to be able to use better judgment.

If you offer a comfortable learning experience when your teen goofs, he or she can learn more quickly from the mistakes and perhaps not repeat them. It would be unrealistic to have a mistake-free teenager as your goal. But you can work to turn mistakes into learning and growing experiences for all of you. I used to tell my teen:

The first time it's a mistake.
The second time you aren't listening.
The third time you deserve what you get.
Mistakes happen. They're part of growing up.
But, they shouldn't become a way of life.

CHAPTER 13

Good Teens, Bad Things

All parents have seen the movie, the one in which the teenager from the good home, the nice, well-mannered, good student, roams the nighttime streets doing dastardly deeds. Before the movie is over, all sorts of things happen to bring parents and teenager into conflict and then back together. At the end, the teen professes great remorse and promises, "I'll never do that again, honest. I promise."

In real life, things don't always work out that way. Teenagers are still teenagers. That doesn't change overnight, no matter how grown-up the teen's intentions may be. Sometimes, in spite of the parent's best efforts, a teenager does walk down an unacceptable road. Temptations are out there. Most parents strive to teach their kids values and standards of behavior. But even the best lessons are forgotten now and then. Things happen. Even the best of teens gets waylaid and knocked off the straight-and-narrow. Sometimes they simply step off the straight-and-narrow. After all, they are teens.

Parents whose kids stray can feel devastated. They tried to give their teenagers morals, ethics, and values. They raised their kids right and taught them to respect law, family, and society. When their teens derail from these tracks, parents can become immobilized, often lashing out without thinking. *How can our teenager do this to us? After all the years of sacrifice...after all the years of being good...Why did this happen to us?*

Drugs, Sex, Alcohol

Temptations of the flesh are everywhere. Drugs, sex, and alcohol are almost interchangeable. Many teens will tell you that if you can't get one, you can get another. This is a line that is easy for teens to step over without thought.

It is usually curiosity far more than rebellion against their parents that leads teens into experimentation and bad habits. Teens often try to live up to the standards set by their parents, but these standards can be ambiguous. Parents often say, "Do this," but what teens hear is, "Do as I say, not as I do." Teens watch their own parents playing loose with these same temptations and wonder why something that is so bad for teens can be perfectly okay for adults.

Pressures to "stray" are considerable. Teens cite peer pressure, teen culture, the urge to figure things out, the lure of getting away with something, and simply the general expectations of themselves and others. Teens are not always able to put temptations into perspective. *I'm only young once....It's not going to happen to me....I can handle it....It's not my fault....That's life....Everybody's doing it.* Teens have all sorts of resources to justify their indulgence in forbidden fruit.

Sometimes, teens need to be "cool." In the teen's eyes, it gets them friends. It helps them negotiate the teenage years successfully and become one of the group. Kevin, for example, was a kid most parents would be proud of. He was an honor's student, president of the student body, active in school activities, and a member of the basketball team. In short, he was a "geek."

Then, Kevin went to a party. Good ol' Kevin had a personality change. He drank. He smoked. He became the life of the party. No one called him a nerd, probably because everyone else was further gone than he was. His new "friends" told him what a swell guy he was. Then the party ended, and Kevin went back to being his normal, geeky self. But now, he was just a little cooler. Fortunately for him, he stopped before anything serious happened.

The desire for acceptance can be powerful. Teens want their peers to know that they can play in the big leagues, just like their friends. "Everyone was sleeping around at fourteen," Rachelle said. "All my friends did. They would ask me when I was going to. I wasn't afraid. It's just that I wanted it to be something special. I knew that sooner or later I'd do it. I finally did with a friend. It was no big deal. We broke up several days later. You know what? Now that I've done it, I can live without him. The pressure is off from my friends, too. It's messing up my current relationship a little, but what's done is done and can't be undone."

Often, teens speak of their experiences as if they had happened to someone else. They don't always feel connected to what happened, almost as if they were trying to deny that they did it or that it made any difference at all. Bad experiences in particular are easy to forget if they can be made into something remote and disconnected to reality. Hard luck becomes the stand-in for naiveté and recklessness.

When things happen that even teens consider bad, they often blame someone else so they can make themselves innocent and someone else responsible. Perhaps it is a formerly trusted friend or a nogoodnick acquaintance. The teen is just an innocent victim, someone who was in the wrong place at the wrong time or someone whose trust was violated. Shirley, for example, accepted her best friend's invitation to a party. It was no problem that there would be drinking, dancing, and partying until the late hours. Lois, her friend, promised her a safe place to sleep.

This "safe place" was the back of Lois' boyfriend's flatbed truck. It was cool, Lois promised, because her boyfriend wasn't interested in Shirley. Yeah, right. "Her so-called boyfriend rolled over on to me, then he wouldn't get up. I tried to fight him off, but I was too drunk. It was awful. He wouldn't get off, and I was scared. I felt betrayed. Finally, he just rolled off, too skunked to get it on, I guess. I'll never trust Lois again. Some safe place to sleep she gave me!"

Some kids learn from their first big mistakes. Some don't. Shirley was so scared by what happened that she ended up making the same mistake all over again a few months later.

Who or What Is in Control?

Teens are not always the best caretakers of their own interests. It is easy to be blinded by temporary feelings or the misconception of the moment. Andrianne, for example, chose to become anorexic because the girl's magazines she read all conveyed the message that boys were turned on by thin girls and off by fat ones. Then she graduated to bulimia. "I felt guilty whenever I ate something that would make me feel fat or overweight. I started to vomit three times a week, which gave me a high and a certain control over my body that no one could take away from me. I eat just enough to balance everything out, and no one suspects. If I'm careful, no one ever will." (This is not just something girls do; boys do the same thing with the steroids that give them extra muscle for sports and filling in their clothes.)

Albert turned to drugs when he thought his teenage life made too many demands. At the age of fifteen, he began smoking dope a couple of times a week to reduce the stresses of school, parents, and social activities. Or so he said. He said it improved his art; the visions he saw through the dark glasses he seemed to wear all the time really "opened up" his mind. No one agreed. He began slurring his speech, fuzzing up his thinking, turning in assignments late, and generally failing to live up to what others had learned they could expect from him.

By the time he graduated, Albert had added crack to his regimen and experimented with almost anything else he could get his hands on. He took to hanging around the streets, staring at, doing, and, some believed, thinking nothing. His parents tried unsuccessfully three times to offer him medical help. Finally, Albert woke up in downtown Toledo. Someone was rolling him for loose change, and he didn't know how he got there. He returned to the rehab clinic voluntarily and at last cleaned his life up.

Some kids hook up with gangs. These provide the structure and guidance that some teens cannot or will not give themselves. Gangs offer teens identity, belonging, coolness, "badness," and any number of other badges that let teens feel important and invulnerable. Gangs provide at least some teens with a self-image that seems to be more substantial than reality.

Gangs often require that the teen trade membership in the outside world for membership in the gang. Initiation into many gangs, in fact, involves a ritual in which the teen has to prove that the gang is more important than the rest of society. If a teen is lucky, that symbolic choice can mean doing something marginally antisocial, like slaughtering a chicken or shoplifting a trinket or a candy bar. Lots of teens are not lucky. They are pressured to do something serious to prove themselves. In too many places, violence, mayhem, vandalism, even murder have become the dues of gang membership.

So is drug-dealing, a gang-type activity that seems so common that teens feel safe to do it with impunity. The advantages are obvious: the teen's allowance doubles or quadruples and, unless the teen is careless, parents and others never notice the extra cash flowing into and out of the teen's pockets. This extra cash fosters a sense of power and lets the teen feel important, even arrogant. To many of these teens, they're not doing anything wrong. They're just local business people providing a service to the community. Perhaps we should thank them.

What makes gangs and reckless behavior such problems for the rest of society is that they work. They provide certain teens with what they think is a good life. They offer a sense of identity, importance, and membership that some teens, for whatever reason, cannot get or refuse to accept from the larger society. The fact that there are kids who do not join gangs makes no difference. To teens who are gang members, gang behavior makes perfect sense, and normal behavior is perfectly wimpy.

Putting It In Perspective

Certainly, parents need to do something. But first, they need to understand what is going on in the mind of their teenager.

The first thing to remember is this: it is not personal. Your teenager didn't deliberately set out to ruin your life. Teenagers don't always think or reason things through. They are impulsive. They see things in black and white. There are few gray tones, and those that do exist are not defined very well. This area remains in the shadows even for the teen, who understandably does not feel comfortable in this unexplored and unexamined territory of uncertainty.

Second, teenagers think in terms of "immediately." Whatever they do is likely to be a short-term solution to a right-now problem. Teens seldom think about the long-term consequences of what they're doing. They don't usually look very far down the road. That's one reason why they still live at home, where there are parents to solve problems and take care of them.

Third, teenagers often forget that their actions reflect back on or involve their parents and others. Teenagers act as egos unto themselves. Often, they don't consider and sometimes don't care that other people may be affected by what they do or how they do it. They don't look that far outside themselves.

(When my teenager got his first speeding ticket, for example, it never occurred to him that the judge might suspend his license, make him pay a fine, or even appear in court or that I might be affected by his punishment. It turned out that the judge did all three, and my son's punishment became mine. I did get even, though. I made him bike to many of his appointments and pay his own fine, the equivalent of four months' allowance. He suffered at least as much as I did.)

Fourth, teenagers don't usually recognize when they are doing something wrong. In their minds, solutions are simple and absolute. "There is no other way to proceed or to make it better....It's the only way to accomplish what I am trying to accomplish....There is the problem and here is the simple solution." Teenagers may lack the experience that leads to good judgment, but that doesn't prevent them from expecting you to challenge the solutions that are so obvious to them. So, knowing that they are right and expecting to be criticized, they keep secrets.

Finally, no matter how ticked off you become at your teenager, keep your composure. Count to twenty-five in Swahili if it's going to calm your temper down. This may not be easy to do, as my bedroom pillow will evidence. But getting angry and riffling through your teenager's belongings is not acceptable adult behavior. Treat your teenager at least as well as you'd treat your spouse. Sit down and have a talk with yourself. Understand why you're angry and then decide how to handle the situation. Don't just attack. Don't just accuse. Don't hit. If your relationship with your child is important to you (and it is, isn't it?), don't undermine it by acting rashly or impulsively.

Your Kid's On Drugs

Don't expect your teenager to march into the dining room one evening and proudly announce: "Mom, Dad, I'm doing drugs!" Chances are that you are going to have to figure this out for yourself. Most of the time, kids on drugs will give themselves away. Some of the more common tell-tale signs are: school and social failures; attitude and behavior changes; negativity; loss of values, and forceful denial. Drug use usually begins between the ages of ten and thirteen, though it can start at virtually any time.

An important clue may lie in *your* behavior. There is a fine line between what a teenager does and what a parent does. Consider the kind of influence you are on your teenager. Are you a social drinker? Do you use alcohol to settle your nerves? If so, your teen probably got the message from you that it is okay to use alcohol in this manner. Do you smoke grass or use other substances? Chances are that your teenager will do it, too. Take a look at the messages you are sending to your kids.

If you still think your teenager is involved with drugs, take the following steps before you act drastically:

☞ Have your teen examined by your regular doctor or, prefer- ably, by a substance-abuse specialist who is better in- formed about indications than a general practitioner.

☞ Ask for an assessment of your teen's recent performance and behavior in school. Request input from teachers, who may have considerable daily involvement with your teen- ager.

☞ Always get a second opinion.

Your Responsibility

Many teens who go astray have relationship and commu- nication problems with their parents. At some point ear- lier in their teen years (if not before), they lost the ability to talk with their parents. "They wouldn't understand," or, "They've stopped listening to me." These kids are crying out to be heard. Their behavior is the latest scream. These are the teens who most need to establish or rees- tablish communication with their parents. These are the parents who most need to reach out to their kids.

This may be easier to say than it is to do. Often teen and parent alike look the other way when a difficult or painful dialogue is needed. Instead of setting a good ex- ample, too many parents go back to the bottle or the reefer or the outside authorities and deny more loudly than their kids that anything is wrong. Some just don't want to see what is really happening with their kids or acknowledge that darling Jack or Jill is capable of doing bad things. Some parents even encourage their kids to go to ex- cess—it may be the only way they know to view their teens as "successful."

Everyone makes mistakes and does bad things. That is how most people learn some of the rules of social behavior. Drinking, drugs, guns, graffiti, date rape—these are just some of the behaviors showing that teens still have some learning to do about making choices, communicating with their parents, and taking responsibility for their actions. They are also symptoms that parents have some work of their own to do.

Teens don't go bad intentionally, and a bad deed does not make a bad person. Teens stray because it seems the easier choice at the time. Most teens have learned to do this from watching their parents. If parents make poor choices or take the easy way out, their teens are likely to handle situations in the same way. If their parents habitually use bad judgment or uncommon sense, teens have no other role models to follow. If parents face what needs to be confronted, teens learn that taking responsibility may not be pleasant, but it is the way things need to be done.

Teens also stray when they feel their parents don't care. Without parental support and involvement, it becomes much easier for teens to go off in their own directions. Teens lack the experience and insight of their parents; whose fault is it really if parents have failed to share their wisdom with their teens?

Teens are going to test, to stray, to yield to temptations. Some may stray permanently. More are likely to try out temptations once or twice and then return to more approved ways of being. Take it in stride. Straying only becomes a problem when it becomes a pattern of behavior instead of a momentary lapse or a passing infatuation.

How much and how far teenagers will stray depends in large measure on how much their parents are parts of their lives. When they do lapse, many teens are more upset by their inability to speak with and confide in their parents than by the the particular trouble they may have made for themselves. The closer parents are to their teens and the more interest parents take in their children's lives, the less likely it is that their teens will stray beyond the point of redemption.

CHAPTER 14

Some Parting Advice

*When I was a boy of fourteen, my father was so ignorant I
could hardly stand to have the old man around. But when
I got to be twenty-one I was astonished at how much the
old man had learned in seven years.* ... Mark Twain

The teenage years only seem endless. Sooner or later,
your teen is going to say, "So long, folks," and run out the
front door. When that happens, you will join the ever-
growing crowd of parents who have survived the trials and
tribulations of the teenage years without permanently
losing their cool.

Successful parents of teenagers conquered the bewildering years without necessarily understanding why these
years are so bewildering. Like their fellow survivors everywhere, these parents learn to balance and coordinate the
often conflicting demands of authority, direction, freedom, choice, communication, and relationships that so
dominate the teenage years. They work with their teens,
even if reluctantly, to make sure that their teens are able
to move into a world made up of adults, all of whom were
teenagers once themselves.

Successful parents learn humility. If they thought
they were perfect before they had a teenager, their expe-

riences quickly disabuse them of the notion. Dealing with their teens, they realize, is dealing with themselves. Teens become mirrors of their parents, reflecting all the strengths and flaws that make the parents human. At the same time, teens demonstrate all the personal characteristics that make them unique individuals. Shepherding a teenager into adulthood is often difficult and thankless. It is a wonder that so many parents persevere to the end.

But persevere they do. While they are persevering, most successful parents learn a few basic lessons about parenting teens:

- ☞ Be consistent and have a plan. Present a unified front with your spouse and others who help give direction to your teen's growth.
- ☞ Be definitive. Lay down the rules and let your teen know what they are.
- ☞ Be authoritative, not arbitrary. Make your rules appropriate for your teen. Younger teens need more structure, older teens more space.
- ☞ Be willing to discipline. Teens need to learn to discipline themselves, but until they do, you need to provide them with discipline from the outside.
- ☞ Be in control. You, the parent, need to have authority and be willing to assert it.
- ☞ Be open. Teens communicate and relate in their own ways, which may not be their parents' ways. Meet your teen half-way so you both can understand each other.
- ☞ Be helpful. Give feedback. Send the right messages, and make sure that your teen receives them correctly.
- ☞ Be open-minded. Don't simply confront your teen. Let your teen tell the truth in his or her own ways. Don't condemn without knowing all the facts.
- ☞ Be present. Take the time to find out who your teen is at any given moment. Your teen is changing rapidly, becoming an individual and not a clone of anyone else.

☞ Be flexible. Let your teen make choices, even if you do not agree with them. Give your child the luxury of making mistakes while you are still there to pick him or her up.

☞ Be venturesome. Enlarge your teen's realm of freedom as your teen grows older and let your teen learn how to handle freedom while still living at home.

☞ Be a role-model. Your teen is observing you and copying what you do. Set a good example.

☞ Be understanding. Teens go through stages, just like everyone else. Give your teen the space to experience each stage and the structure to handle his or her own behavior.

☞ Be instructive. Give your teen every opportunity to learn from experiences and mistakes. Help your teen learn that actions have consequences that need to be taken into consideration.

☞ Be a facilitator. Give your teen every opportunity to move toward independence. Be there in case the road gets bumpy. As difficult as it may be, rejoice when your teen gets there.

Being the parent of a teenager does not just happen. It is built on the foundation you started to construct when your teen was a small child. Don't wait for the first sign that a teenager is emerging to start mixing the mortar. By then, it may be too late to save the therapist's fees.

There is no way of predicting what your teen may do. Teen behavior has as much variety as any part of social life. Different teens respond differently to the same stimuli and mature at vastly different speeds. But all teens have a few things in common. You can take comfort that your teen is not acting weird. Your teen is just being a teenager!

Index

Alcohol   160
Authority   6-7, 12, 15- 24, 31
Autonomy   6-7, 25-26
  SEE ALSO Direction

Bookbags   124

Choice   8-9, 10, 12, 35-50, 53
Clothing   37-39
Communication   10-12, 17-19,
  20, 57, 65-72
Concrete steps
  SEE Testing
Conditioned manipulation
  115-117
Consequences   9, 49, 59-62
Control
  SEE Authority, Direction
Cooperation   32-33

Dating   83-85
Direction   7-8, 12, 25-33
  External   25
  Internal   25
Discipline   29-30
  SEE ALSO Direction
Doorways   136
  SEE ALSO Playrooms
Drugs   160, 166-167

Etiquette
  SEE Manners
Evasion   111-112, 123

Fairness   16-17
Fairness   7, 16

Fait Accompli   107
Flexibility   28-29
Food   43-45
Freedom   7, 9-10, 12, 25, 51-63
Friendships   12, 39, 80
  Confidential   80
  Just-between-friends   80
  Opposite-sex   83

Gangs   163-164
Guidance   21, 30
  SEE ALSO Authority, Direction

Hair   37-38
Home Alone Manual   78-79
Homework   47-49

Independence   25
  SEE ALSO Direction

Lipping off   67-69

Mail   126-127
Manipulation   103-118
  and Consequences   113
  and Guilt   105
  and Parents   107
  and Relatives   109
  and Sympathy   106
  of parents   107-109
Manners   45-47
Mistakes   9, 139-140, 149- 157
  and ignorance   151-152
  and inattention   152-153
  and poor judgment   150-151
  Compound   155-156

Obedience   15-16, 19-21, 139
One-liners   93
    SEE ALSO Communication
    Lipping off

Peer pressure   20, 160
Picking fights   110
Playrooms   135-148
    And Parents   145-148
    and Relationships   143-144
    and Responsibility   140-143
Privacy   119-133
    and Bathrooms   121
    and Bedrooms   121-122
    and personal property   124-
    127
    and Respect   127-129
    and Restaurants   122-123
    Invasions of   129-133
    Outside   122
Procrastination   110-111

Relationships   12-13, 73-88
    Family   74-76
    Evolution of   73
Respect   7
    and Communication   11, 71
    and Discipline   31
    SEE ALSO Authority
Responsibility   9, 53, 62-63
    and parents   167-168

Role models   26-27
Rubber steps
    SEE Testing

School   47-49, 86-87
School Papers   124
Self-direction
    SEE Direction
Self-discipline
    SEE Direction
Self-esteem   8, 27, 33
Sex   85-86, 160
Sibling Trail   75
Social skills   18
Support   30-31

Teachers   86-87
Telephones   100-101, 125-126
Testing   89-102
    and Failure   99-100
    and Responsibility   100-101
    and Rules   97-99
    and Strategy   94-95
    Evolution of   91-92
Trust   22, 57

Ultimatums   21-22
    SEE ALSO Authority
Unacceptable manipulation
    117-118

Other Books from Silvercat Publications

How to Be Smart Parents Now That Your Kids Are Adults, by Sylvia Auerbach (ISBN 0-9624945-8-5, $14.95). *A wise, practical guide to the rewards and challenges of being parents to grown children.*

Who Do You Want to Be? The Art of Presenting Yourself With Ease, by Glynn Bedington (ISBN 0-9624945-9-3, $10.95). *Information, exercises, and encouragement from one of the country's premier presentation trainers.*

Moving: A Complete Checklist and Guide for Relocation, by Karen G. Adams (ISBN 0-9624945-6-9, $8.95). *Checklists, tips, and ideas from a veteran of 30 moves.*

PLEASE SEND ME:

____ copies of *Teenagers! A Bewildered Parent's Guide,* at $11.95 each.

____ copies of *How To Be Smart Parents Now That Your Kids Are Adults*, at $14.95 each.

____ copies of *Who Do You Want To Be: The Art of Presenting Yourself with Ease*, at $10.95 each.

____ copies of *Moving: A Complete Checklist and Guide for Relocation*, at $8.95 each.

Name _____

Address _____

_____

City _____ State, ZIP _____

Please check the appropriate boxes:

❏ **Payment enclosed.** Amount $_____ (*California residents, please add 7% sales tax.*)

❏ **Please bill my:** ❏ VISA ❏ MasterCard ❏ AMEX ❏ Optima

Account No. _____ Expires _____

Name on card _____

Daytime phone _____

Signature _____

Order from

Silvercat Publications
4070 Goldfinch St., Suite C
San Diego, CA 92103-1865
619-299-6774 / 299-9119 (fax)